THE   BOOK   OF

ONE-POT
COOKING

T H E   B O O K   O F

ONE-POT
COOKING

MARY READER

Foreword by
BRIAN TURNER,
top TV chef

Photographed by
SIMON BUTCHER

a Salamander book

Published by Salamander Books Limited
LONDON

Published by Salamander Books Limited
129-137 York Way, London N7 9LG, United Kingdom

9 8 7 6 5 4 3 2 1

© Salamander Books Ltd., 1996

ISBN 0-86101-814-1

Produced by ZEBU
Editor: Vicky Hanson
Art Director: Vicky Zentner
Photographer: Simon Butcher
Photographer's Assistant: David Baird
Home Economist: Nicola Fowler
Home Economist's Assistant: Liz Comben
Stylist: Shannon Beare
Colour separation: Classic Scan Pte. Ltd., Singapore
Printed in Belgium by Proost International Book Production

Brian Turner's recipes are featured on pages
12, 19, 28, 35, 46, 49, 58, 59, 66, 73, 75, 80, 84, 87, 88, 91, 97,
107, 115, 119.

Notes:
All spoon measurements are level.
1 teaspoon = 5 ml spoon.
1 tablespoon = 15 ml spoon.

CONTENTS

COMPANION VOLUMES OF INTEREST

FOREWORD

'One-pot cooking' will always bring back fond memories of my days immediately after catering college. I came to London to live away from home for the first time: it was such an adventure, but not without it's problems! The decisions about what to eat, when to eat and where to eat were always centred on the economics of time and money, as is so often the case today. 'One-pot cooking' provided the answer - no real washing up, and what a treat the last spoonfuls from the pot were!

Thirty years later, with my busy life-style, the need to prepare dishes that are not too time consuming is still important to me. I can prepare most of the dishes in this book in advance, freeze them if necessary, and reheat as and when I need to. What is more, the flavours mature and improve on keeping.

Cooking lots of ingredients in one pot creates dishes that merge together many different flavours. Those of us that love to cook find it so exciting to be able to experiment with dishes like these, which hardly ever fail!

Here we have a collection of dishes that bring together inventiveness, quality and the tradition of good cooking. I hope you enjoy them as much as I have.

COOKING IN ONE POT

All of the dishes in this book can be prepared using only one piece of cookware. One-pot cooking has many advantages, producing tasty, nutritious meals for people from all walks of life, from busy people with families to feed to those with limited cooking facilities. Not only convenient, it also cuts down on washing up and reduces fuel costs, as most of the dishes require only one source of heat.

A flameproof dish or casserole allows you to brown foods on the hob before transferring them to the oven.

ONE-POT RECIPES

The recipes in this book have been chosen to reflect a wide range of cooking styles and use easily available ingredients from all over the world. Many different cooking methods are used, including boiling, grilling, roasting, baking or braising, to show how versatile one-pot cooking can be.

In many of the recipes the meat and vegetables are browned or softened first on top of the cooker before being cooked slowly and gently. Browning meat is not essential, but it does deepen the colour of the sauce, while vegetables take on a sweeter flavour if they are sautéed in a little oil or butter first. Long gentle cooking gives the meat a special tenderness and brings out its flavour to the full, while the vegetables and other ingredients add their goodness to the juices.

Marinating is also sometimes used in the recipes. Again, this is not essential but it does add moisture to lean meats which can be rather dry, and it is also good for tenderizing tougher cuts of meat.

CHOOSING COOKWARE

Investing in good quality cookware is well worthwhile. There are so many different materials and styles available, it can be very difficult to know which one to choose, particularly if you are to rely on only one or two items.

When buying cookware it is important to be aware of the difference between flameproof and ovenproof items as some pieces of equipment can only be used with one source of heat. Because of the techniques employed in one-pot cooking, it is best to choose cookware that is suitable for using both on the hob and in the oven. This is more economical too, as you only need to buy one piece of equipment instead of two. Always buy the best you can afford: better materials give better cooking results and cheaper items only have to be replaced after a short time.

FLAMEPROOF COOKWARE

Many recipes require you to start cooking on top of the cooker and then continue in the oven or under the grill. It is therefore essential that you choose a cooking container for this purpose that is flameproof as well as ovenproof. A dish or casserole which is only ovenproof would buckle or break if used on the hob.

A flameproof casserole can receive direct heat through its base. For this reason it should have a flat, stable base. If it is too thin, the food being cooked in it is apt to burn and the pan may buckle. In addition, the material used to make the pan must be able to conduct the heat evenly from the base to the rest of the pan.

The most popular choices for flameproof cookware are made of cast iron or enamel-coated cast iron. These are usually very heavy and fairly deep with straight sides. They conduct heat evenly and gently and are particularly good for dishes that require long, slow cooking. But although they give good cooking results, their weight means they are not an ideal choice for anyone who cannot lift heavy objects.

If you are looking for something lighter, then glass ceramic cookware is an excellent choice. It is both flameproof and ovenproof and can also be used under the grill.

Hard anodised aluminium dishes and casseroles are also flameproof and ovenproof. They are durable, hard-wearing and completely unbreakable. Some have handles which are only suitable for using in the oven at low temperatures, but they are often adequate for casserole cooking. Others have handles made of metal and so will withstand higher temperatures. Many of these pans have a non-stick coating which is extremely easy to clean.

Stainless steel pans with a soundly bonded aluminium base are also very good. Some of these have a non-stick coating, tough enough to allow you to use metal tools, and easy to clean. Always check the manufacturer's instructions before buying, to ensure that the dish can be used on the hob.

OVENPROOF COOKWARE

When baking or roasting, the heat conductor is the air inside the oven. This means that cookware which is only to be used in the oven does not have to be such a good conductor of heat as it does if it is to go on the hob. A much wider range of materials are therefore suitable. Cast iron, copper, aluminium, glass ceramic, glass and earthenware are all efficient, but it is worth noting that metal is the best conductor of heat and it may be necessary to increase cooking times given in a recipe if you are using ceramic or glass cookware.

The size of an ovenproof dish is crucial. If it is too large, the juices or liquid in the dish could evaporate too quickly or even burn. If the dish is too small, the food may spill over the sides during cooking. Any lids should fit snugly to keep the moisture inside and prevent the food from drying out.

There is a vast range of cookware available. Choose wisely and you will need only a couple of items to produce everything from casseroles and roasts to gratins and puddings.

COOKING ON THE HOB

For best results when cooking on the hob, place the pot over a medium heat to ensure that the outer part does not heat up too quickly, and to give good, even cooking without burning. Food could stick to the bottom if too much heat is applied too quickly. Non-stick pans should not be used over high temperatures as this may reduce the effectiveness of the coating.

♦ Do not allow gas flames to lick up the sides of the pan as this wastes energy - the useful heat is that applied to the base.

♦ Choose a boiling ring similar in size to the base of the pan to make efficient use of the heat.

A large dish or pan is vital for stir-frying as it allows plenty of room for turning the ingredients.

♦ When cooking casseroles, vegetables or pasta dishes, half-fill the pan with the cooking liquid so that it is about three-quarters full when all of the ingredients are added. This ensures that there is enough space for the food to move freely around in the liquid and to cook evenly.

♦ Always make sure that both the base of the pan and the hob are clean and dry before use. This is particularly important when using a glass ceramic or halogen hob. Dampness can cause spitting and affect the efficiency of the hob. Some ceramic hobs will turn themselves off if the base of the pan is too damp.

♦ When using a ceramic or halogen hob avoid dragging the pan over the surface and be careful not to drop it on to the hob as this could damage the hob permanently.

♦ Try to avoid dragging a pan over a gas hob, too, as pan supports on some cookers can be a little unstable.

COOKING UNDER THE GRILL

Grilling is often used as a healthier alternative to frying, but the direct heat of a grill is also useful for browning the tops of dishes such as gratins after they have been cooked in the oven. Many cookers have the grill in the top of the oven so you may have to adjust the position of the top shelf.

♦ For best results, always preheat the grill for 5 minutes before using. This enables the surface of the grill to become evenly heated all over and to reach a steady temperature.

♦ Place the dish at least 7.5 cm (3 ins) from the surface of the grill so the heat can distribute itself evenly over the surface of the food.

COOKING IN THE OVEN

Ovens give a gentle heat, ideal for braising and casseroles.

♦ Preheat the oven for 10 minutes before use, to ensure it has reached the correct temperature and that the temperature is steady.

♦ Remember that ovens can vary enormously in the way they work so be prepared to adjust the temperatures given in the recipes to suit your oven.

♦ All cooking temperatures in the recipes are for standard ovens. If you have a forced convection (fan-assisted) oven, the temperature and cooking time should be reduced: consult the manufacturer's handbook for advice on your particular model.

♦ In standard ovens the top is always the hottest. Unless otherwise stated in a recipe, the dish should be placed on the middle shelf. In forced convection ovens the air is constantly circulating, so the temperature is even throughout.

COOKING IN A MICROWAVE

Although the recipes in this book give instructions for conventional ovens and hobs, many can be adapted for the microwave or at least partly cooked in it. A microwave can also be used for thawing and reheating frozen dishes.

♦ Never put metallic containers in a microwave. Some glass ceramic dishes can be transferred straight from the freezer, but be sure to check the manufacturer's handbook first.

♦ Remember to stir foods frequently during microwaving, to ensure they are properly heated throughout, particularly if the food has been frozen. It is vital that food reaches a high enough temperature to kill bacteria that causes food poisoning.

COOKING FOR THE FREEZER

Most of the recipes in this book are suitable for freezing. If you make larger quantities than you actually need, you can freeze the remainder for another day, saving time and energy.

• It is a good idea to freeze in small, manageable quantities, such as one or two portions at a time, rather than large blocks. The food is not only easier to thaw this way, it allows you to be more flexible and cater for any number of people.

• Certain flavours may intensify when frozen, so if you are cooking specifically for the freezer you should use smaller amounts of herbs and spices. Frozen dishes containing spices, garlic and salty foods should be eaten within six weeks.

• Most foods freeze well but avoid freezing mayonnaise (unless it is in a mousse), bananas and avocados (they discolour), full-fat milk and cream (although it will freeze if it is whipped first). Foods with a high water content such as lettuce and strawberries become soft when thawed. Raw egg yolks and/or whites will freeze, but hard-boiled eggs will not.

• Make sure that you wrap foods well before freezing. Food will dry out in the freezer if the packing is not airtight. Wrapping materials should be thicker

Cookware that can be taken straight to the table for serving is always useful, so choose items that look as good in the dining room as they do in the kitchen.

than normal and strong enough not to tear easily. Containers with sealable lids are ideal for freezing, especially square ones which pack easily.

• Liquids expand on freezing, so packaging of dishes such as soups and foods with a sauce needs to allow for this. Fill the container to within 2.5 cm (1 in) of the top and do not seal until the food is frozen.

• Always label and date the food. It is very easy to forget exactly what you have frozen after a few weeks, and some foods look very similar when they have been frozen.

• Make sure that all cooked dishes are reheated thoroughly before serving.

FROM OVEN TO TABLE

Ovenproof dishes can also be used for serving the food cooked in them, so bear this in mind when buying new cookware. Enamelled cast iron, glass ceramic and earthenware can all make attractive serving dishes. Remember that the dish will be very hot when it comes out of the oven, so have a thick mat on the table to prevent the pan from marking it.

—— BEAN & BACON SOUP ——

175 g (6 oz/¾ cup) white haricot beans, soaked
    overnight
1 litre (35 fl oz/4½ cups) chicken stock
115 g (4 oz) smoked streaky bacon, chopped
1 Cos lettuce, shredded
2 egg yolks
150 ml (5 fl oz/⅔ cup) crème fraîche
1 tablespoon white wine vinegar
salt and freshly ground black pepper
chopped fresh coriander, to garnish

Drain the beans. Rinse and drain again. Put into a large flameproof casserole and cover with cold water. Bring to the boil, skimming the scum from the surface. Drain.

Return the beans to the casserole, add the stock and bring to the boil. Add the bacon and simmer for 1½ hours, until the beans are tender, topping up with water if necessary. Remove about half of the beans with a slotted spoon and roughly mash them. Return to the soup and stir well. Add the lettuce and simmer for 15 minutes.

In a bowl, mix together the egg yolks, crème fraîche and vinegar. Add to the soup and heat gently, stirring, until warmed through. Season with salt and pepper. Garnish with chopped coriander and serve.

Serves 6-8.

ROAST PARSNIP SOUP

450 g (1 lb) parsnips, cut into chunks
1 tablespoon olive oil
salt and freshly ground black pepper
1 large potato, cut into chunks
1 large onion, chopped
850 ml (30 fl oz/3¾ cups) vegetable stock
2 tablespoons Greek yogurt
large pinch of freshly grated nutmeg
Greek yogurt and freshly grated nutmeg, to garnish

Arrange the parsnips in the bottom of a large flameproof casserole. Drizzle with the oil and season with salt and pepper.

Cook very gently for 15-20 minutes, turning once, until browned all over. Add the potato and onion and cook, stirring occasionally, for 10 minutes. Add the stock, bring to the boil and simmer for 35 minutes.

Purée the soup in a blender or food processor and return to the casserole. Stir in the yogurt, nutmeg and salt and pepper and heat gently to warm through. Pour into warmed serving plates, swirl in a little yogurt, sprinkle with nutmeg and serve.

Serves 4-6.

—BROCCOLI & CHEESE SOUP—

225 g (8 oz) broccoli
1 tablespoon sunflower oil
1 leek, thinly sliced
175 g (6 oz) potatoes, diced
salt and freshly ground black pepper
500 ml (18 fl oz/2 ¼ cups) chicken stock
150 ml (5 fl oz/⅔ cup) dry white wine
115 g (4 oz/1 cup) grated Cheddar cheese

Cut the stems from the broccoli flowerets
and cut into 1 cm (½ in) pieces. Heat the oil
in a flameproof casserole.

Add the leek, potatoes and broccoli and
cook, stirring occasionally, for 5 minutes.
Season generously with salt and pepper. Add
the stock and white wine and bring to the
boil. Simmer for 20 minutes, until the
vegetables are tender.

Purée in a blender or food processor and
return to the casserole. Add the cheese,
reserving a little for garnish, and heat gently,
stirring, until the cheese is thoroughly melted
into the soup. Garnish with the reserved
grated cheese and serve.

Serves 4.

Note: Do not allow the soup to boil after
you add the cheese or it will become stringy.

—— BEEF & KIDNEY BEAN SOUP ——

1 tablespoon olive oil
3 onions, chopped
450 g (1 lb) lean minced beef
3 cloves garlic, crushed
1 teaspoon dried thyme
1 teaspoon paprika
2 teaspoons tomato purée (paste)
425 g (15 oz) can red kidney beans, drained
850 ml (30 fl oz/3¾ cups) beef stock
300 ml (10 fl oz/1¼ cups) tomato juice
1 teaspoon cayenne pepper
2 tablespoons chopped fresh parsley
salt

Heat the oil in a large flameproof casserole. Add the onions and minced beef.

Cook gently, stirring and breaking up the mince, until the onions are soft and the mince is browned all over. Add the garlic, thyme, paprika and tomato purée (paste). Cook gently for 5 minutes, stirring constantly. Stir in the beans, stock and tomato juice.

Bring to the boil, cover and simmer gently for 10 minutes. Add the cayenne pepper and half the parsley and season with salt. Garnish with the remaining parsley and serve.

Serves 6-8.

TUSCAN BEAN SOUP

1 tablespoon olive oil
1 bunch spring onions, chopped
2 carrots, diced
2 sticks celery, sliced
2 parsnips, diced
115 g (4 oz) swede, diced
115 g (4 oz) turnips, diced
2 bay leaves
1 litre (35 fl oz/4½ cups) chicken stock or water
55 g (2 oz) macaroni
400 g (14 oz) can cannellini beans, drained
salt and freshly ground black pepper
chopped fresh parsley, to garnish

Heat the oil in a large flameproof casserole.
Add the vegetables and bay leaves.

Cook very gently, stirring occasionally, for
10 minutes, until soft. Add the chicken stock
or water and the macaroni. Bring to the boil
and simmer for 25 minutes. Add the beans
and cook for 5 minutes, to warm through.

Stir well and season with salt and pepper.
Remove and discard the bay leaf. Garnish
with chopped parsley and serve.

Serves 6-8.

— BEETROOT & POTATO SOUP —

1 tablespoon olive oil
1 onion, chopped
225 g (8 oz) potatoes, diced
350 g (12 oz) raw beetroot, diced
1 litre (35 fl oz/4½ cups) chicken stock or water
½ cucumber, diced
bouquet garni
1 tablespoon wine vinegar
1 tablespoon lemon juice
salt and freshly ground black pepper
2 tablespoons thick sour cream

Heat the oil in a large flameproof casserole.
Add the onion and potatoes, and cook,
stirring occasionally, for 5 minutes.

Add the beetroot, stock or water, cucumber,
bouquet garni, vinegar and lemon juice. Bring
to the boil and simmer for 40-50 minutes.

Season generously with salt and pepper. Pour
into warmed serving plates, swirl in the sour
cream and serve.

Serves 6-8.

FRANKFURTER SOUP

1 tablespoon olive oil
1 onion, chopped
55 g (2 oz) streaky bacon, chopped
1 small white cabbage, shredded
225 g (8 oz) carrots, sliced
450 g (1 lb) potatoes, diced
1 litre (35 fl oz/4½ cups) vegetable stock
350 g (12 oz) frankfurters, cut into four
large pinch of freshly grated nutmeg
salt and freshly ground black pepper
3 tablespoons fromage frais

Heat the oil in a large flameproof casserole. Add the onion and bacon and cook gently, stirring occasionally, for 5 minutes.

Add the cabbage, carrots, potatoes and vegetable stock. Bring to the boil and simmer gently for 15 minutes.

Add the frankfurters and simmer gently for 10 minutes. Season with nutmeg and salt and pepper. Stir in the fromage frais and heat gently to warm through. Serve.

Serves 6-8.

——— FISH & MUSSEL CHOWDER ———

1 tablespoon olive oil
2 rashers streaky bacon, cut into fine strips
1 large onion, finely chopped
2 potatoes, diced
450 ml (16 fl oz/2 cups) chicken stock
450 g (1 lb) smoked haddock, skinned and cubed
55 g (2 oz/½ cup) plain flour
20 mussels, scrubbed and trimmed
300 ml (10 fl oz/1¼ cups) crème fraîche
salt and freshly ground black pepper
2 tablespoons chopped fresh parsley

Heat the oil in a large flameproof casserole.
Add the bacon and cook, stirring, until crisp.
Add the onion, potatoes and stock.

Bring to the boil, cover and simmer gently
for 15 minutes, until the potatoes are tender.
Coat the haddock with the flour, shaking off
the excess. Add to the casserole with the
mussels. Add the crème fraîche and heat
gently for 3-4 minutes until the mussels open.
Discard any mussels that remain closed.

Season with salt and pepper and stir in half
the parsley. Garnish with the remaining
parsley and serve.

Serves 4-6.

-CHICKEN LIVERS WITH MANGO-

1 tablespoon olive oil
1 small onion, chopped
350 g (12 oz) chicken livers, trimmed
300 ml (10 fl oz/1¼ cups) low fat fromage frais
2 teaspoons Worcestershire sauce
2 teaspoons wholegrain mustard
1 mango, sliced
basil sprigs, to garnish

Heat the oil in a flameproof casserole. Add the onion and cook, stirring occasionally, for 5 minutes, until soft. Add the chicken livers and cook, stirring, for 5 minutes.

In a small bowl, mix together the fromage frais, Worcestershire sauce and mustard. Pour over the chicken livers in the casserole.

Add the mango slices and cook gently, stirring, for 2 minutes. Garnish with basil sprigs and serve immediately.

Serves 4.

BAKED COURGETTES

4 courgettes (zucchini)
115 g (4 oz) cooked smoked ham, chopped
175 g (6 oz) goats' cheese, softened
175 g (6 oz) button mushrooms, finely chopped
25 g (1 oz/¼ cup) walnuts, chopped
¼ teaspoon freshly grated nutmeg
salt and freshly ground black pepper
115 g (4 oz/1 cup) grated Emmental cheese
flat-leaf parsley sprigs, to garnish

Preheat oven to 180C (350F/Gas 4). Cut the courgettes (zucchini) lengthways in half and arrange in a single layer, cut side up, in a shallow ovenproof dish.

In a bowl, mix together the ham, goats' cheese, mushrooms and walnuts. Stir in the nutmeg and season with salt and pepper.

Spread the mixture evenly over the top of the courgettes (zucchini). Sprinkle the Emmental cheese over the top and bake for 30 minutes, until the cheese is melted and golden. Garnish with flat-leaf parsley and serve.

Serves 4.

──HOT CHINESE BEEF SALAD──

finely pared rind and juice of 1 orange
1 clove garlic, crushed
4 tablespoons cider vinegar
3 tablespoons hoisin sauce
1 tablespoon clear honey
700 g (1½ lb) rump steak, cut into thin strips
2 teaspoons sesame oil
225 g (8 oz) chanterelle mushrooms
225 g (8 oz) bean sprouts
salt and freshly ground black pepper
250 g (9 oz) mixed salad leaves
orange twists, to garnish

In a bowl, mix together the orange rind and juice, garlic, cider vinegar, hoisin sauce and honey. Add the rump steak and stir until evenly coated. Cover and chill overnight. Remove the beef from the marinade with a slotted spoon and drain on kitchen paper. Heat the oil in a flameproof casserole. Add the chanterelle mushrooms and cook, stirring occasionally, for 4 minutes, until golden brown. Remove with a slotted spoon and keep warm.

Add the beef, in batches, and cook, stirring, for 4 minutes, until browned and cooked through. Return all the beef, mushrooms and marinade to the pan and bring to the boil, stirring. Add the bean sprouts and salt and pepper and cook, stirring, for 2 minutes. Arrange the salad leaves on individual serving plates and spoon the beef, vegetables and juices at the side. Garnish with orange twists and serve.

Serves 4.

──MUSSELS IN WHITE WINE──

1 tablespoon olive oil
1 small onion, finely chopped
2 plum tomatoes, peeled, seeded and chopped
pinch of chilli powder
500 ml (18 fl oz/2¼ cups) dry white wine
1.35 kg (3 lb) mussels, scrubbed and trimmed
salt and freshly ground black pepper
1 tablespoon chopped fresh flat-leaf parsley

Heat the oil in a large flameproof casserole. Add the onion and cook gently, stirring occasionally, for 5 minutes, until soft. Add the tomatoes, chilli powder and white wine.

Bring to the boil. Add the mussels, cover tightly and cook over a high heat, shaking the casserole occasionally, for 3-4 minutes, until the mussels open. Discard any mussels that remain closed.

Season with salt and pepper, sprinkle with the parsley and serve.

Serves 4.

Note: Before cooking the mussels, discard any that are open and do not close when tapped sharply.

—STIR-FRIED GINGER PRAWNS—

1 tablespoon olive oil
1 red onion, sliced
2.5 cm (1 in) piece fresh root ginger, peeled and
   grated
115 g (4 oz) baby sweetcorn
1 fennel bulb, sliced
2 tablespoons lemon juice
salt and freshly ground black pepper
350 g (12 oz) cooked, peeled prawns

Heat the oil in a flameproof casserole. Add the onion and ginger and cook, stirring occasionally, for 3 minutes.

Add the sweetcorn and fennel and cook, stirring occasionally, for 4 minutes, until the vegetables are just tender.

Add the lemon juice and season with salt and pepper. Add the prawns and cook, stirring, for 2 minutes. Serve immediately.

Serves 4.

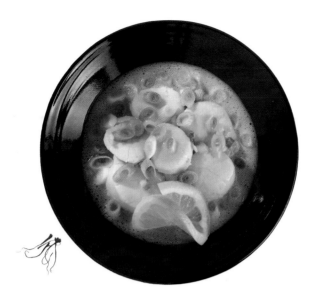

──SCALLOPS WITH LEMON──

4 saffron strands
juice of 1 lemon
1 tablespoon olive oil
8 scallops, sliced
1 bunch spring onions, sliced
1 clove garlic, crushed
salt and freshly ground black pepper
2 teaspoons crème fraîche
lemon twists, to garnish

In a small bowl, soak the saffron in the lemon juice for 1 hour. Heat the oil in a flameproof casserole. Add the scallops and cook, stirring, for 2-3 minutes.

Remove with a slotted spoon and keep warm. Add the spring onions and garlic to the pan and cook gently, stirring occasionally, for 3 minutes, until soft. Strain the lemon juice, discarding the saffron strands. Add the lemon juice to the casserole and stir well to incorporate all the juices.

Season with salt and pepper. Remove from the heat and stir in the crème fraîche. Arrange the scallops on individual serving plates and spoon over the sauce. Garnish with twists of lemon and serve.

Serves 4.

Note: If the scallops still have their roe attached when you buy them, you can use that in the dish, too.

— WARM TROUT & NUT PÂTÉ —

1 tablespoon chopped fresh parsley
115 g (4 oz/1 cup) hazelnuts, chopped
vegetable oil, for greasing
350 g (12 oz) smoked trout fillets, skinned and
    flaked
4 tablespoons fromage frais
salt and freshly ground black pepper
flat-leaf parsley sprigs, to garnish

Preheat oven to 180C (350F/Gas 4). Mix together the parsley and half the hazelnuts. Lightly oil an 850 ml (30 fl oz/3¾ cup) ovenproof dish.

In a bowl, mix together the trout, fromage frais, the remaining hazelnuts and salt and pepper until well blended. Spread half of the trout mixture in the dish. Sprinkle the nut and parsley mixture over the top. Spread the remaining trout mixture on top. Smooth down to level the surface.

Cover the dish with a lid or piece of foil and bake for 20 minutes. Garnish with flat-leaf parsley and serve warm.

Serves 4-6.

— LAYERED TURKEY TERRINE —

8 rashers streaky bacon
450 g (1 lb) minced turkey
225 g (8 oz) pork sausagemeat
115 g (4 oz) chicken livers, trimmed and minced
1 large onion, finely chopped
55 g (2 oz/1 cup) fresh white breadcrumbs
2 tablespoons chopped fresh basil
½ teaspoon salt
¼ teaspoon freshly ground black pepper
1 egg, beaten
3 tomatoes, peeled and sliced
85 g (3 oz) broccoli flowerets, chopped
basil sprigs, to garnish

Stretch the pieces of bacon by gently scraping them with the back of a knife.

Use the bacon rashers to line the base and sides of an 850 ml (30 fl oz/3¾ cup) ovenproof dish. Preheat oven to 180C (350F/ Gas 4). In a bowl, mix together the minced turkey, sausagemeat, chicken livers, onion, breadcrumbs, basil and salt and pepper. Bind together with the egg. Arrange alternate layers of turkey mixture, tomatoes and broccoli in the dish, starting and finishing with the turkey mixture.

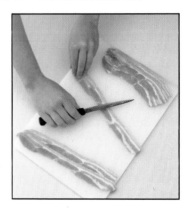

Cover with a lid or foil. Place in a deep roasting tin and pour in enough boiling water to come halfway up the sides of the dish. Cook in the oven for 2 hours, or until a skewer inserted in the centre comes out clean. Drain the excess liquid from the terrine, cover with foil and place a heavy weight on top. Leave to cool. Chill for at least 1-2 hours, preferably overnight. Turn out the terrine and cut into slices. Garnish with basil sprigs and serve.

Serves 4-6.

—BAKED SADDLE OF SALMON—

55 g (2 oz/¼ cup) butter, softened
1 clove garlic, crushed
juice of ½ lemon
2 tablespoons chopped fresh parsley
700 g (1½ lb) saddle of salmon, filleted
1 tablespoon olive oil, plus extra for greasing
6 shallots, chopped
150 ml (5 fl oz/⅔ cup) fish stock
175 ml (6 fl oz/¾ cup) red wine
250 ml (9 fl oz/1 cup) veal stock
salt and freshly ground black pepper

In a small bowl, mix the butter with the garlic, lemon juice and 1 tablespoon of the chopped parsley.

Spread one of the halves of salmon with the butter mixture and sandwich the pieces back together. Wrap tightly in cling film and put in the freezer for about 1 hour, to set. Do not freeze. Preheat oven to 200C (400F/Gas 6). Lightly oil a large piece of foil. Take the salmon out of the cling film and wrap tightly in the foil. Place in a shallow ovenproof dish and cook in the oven for 30 35 minutes. Remove from the dish and keep warm.

Heat the oil in the dish, add the shallots and cook gently, stirring, for 3 minutes, until soft. Add the fish stock and red wine and boil until reduced and syrupy. Add the veal stock and boil to reduce slightly. Add the remaining parsley and season with salt and pepper. Divide the sauce among warmed serving plates. Slice the salmon, place on top of the sauce and serve.

Serves 4.

CHEESY HUSS PIE

700 g (1 ½ lb) huss fillets, skinned and cubed
salt and freshly ground black pepper
4 basil leaves, torn
grated rind and juice of 1 lemon
225 g (8 oz) frozen puff pastry
300 ml (10 fl oz/1 ¼ cups) Greek yogurt
200 g (7 oz) can sweetcorn, drained
115 g (4 oz/1 cup) grated Emmental cheese
basil sprigs, to garnish

Preheat oven to 220C (425F/Gas 7). Put the huss in a shallow flameproof dish. Season with salt and pepper, add the basil and pour over the lemon juice.

Cover with a lid or piece of foil and cook for 10-15 minutes. Meanwhile, allow the pastry to thaw for 10 minutes. Add the lemon rind, Greek yogurt, sweetcorn and cheese to the fish mixture and stir well. Grate the pastry evenly over the top.

Bake for 30-40 minutes, until the topping is crisp and golden brown. Garnish with basil sprigs and serve.

Serves 4-6.

CRISPY FISH HOTPOT

350 g (12 oz) courgettes (zucchini), thinly sliced
2 red dessert apples, cored and thinly sliced
1 large onion, sliced
175 g (6 oz) small green beans, cut into 2.5 cm (1 in)
  lengths
1 teaspoon dried sage
300 ml (10 fl oz/1¼ cups) fish stock
700 g (1½ lb) cod fillet, skinned and cubed
salt and freshly ground black pepper
350 g (12 oz) potatoes with the skins on, thinly sliced
85 g (3 oz/¾ cup) grated Cheddar cheese

Preheat oven to 190C (375F/Gas 5). Arrange layers of courgettes (zucchini), apples, onion and beans in an ovenproof casserole.

Sprinkle with sage and pour in the stock. Cover and cook in the oven for 30 minutes. Remove from the oven, arrange the fish on top and season with salt and pepper.

Arrange the sliced potatoes on top, sprinkle with cheese and bake for 35-40 minutes, until the potatoes are tender and the cheese is melted and golden. Serve.

Serves 4-6.

Variation: Any firm white fish fillets, such as whiting or haddock, can be used instead of cod in this recipe.

KEDGEREE

450 g (1 lb) smoked haddock
2 tablespoons olive oil
1 onion, chopped
350 g (12 oz/1½ cups) easy-cook rice
4 hard-boiled eggs, shelled
2 tablespoons crème fraîche
25 g (1 oz/2 tablespoons) butter
3 tablespoons chopped fresh parsley
salt and freshly ground black pepper

Put the haddock in a flameproof casserole with 850 ml (30 fl oz/3¾ cups) water. Bring to the boil and simmer for 10 minutes, until the fish is tender. Remove the haddock with a slotted spoon and keep warm.

Pour the cooking liquid from the casserole and set aside. Heat the oil in the casserole, add the chopped onion and cook, stirring occasionally, for 5 minutes, until soft. Add the rice and cook, stirring, for 1 minute. Pour the reserved cooking liquid over the rice, bring to the boil, cover and simmer for 15-20 minutes, until the liquid has been absorbed and the rice is tender. Remove from the heat.

Cut the hard-boiled eggs into wedges. Flake the haddock and gently mix into the rice with the eggs, crème fraîche, butter and parsley. Season with salt and pepper. Return to the heat and cook gently for 2-3 minutes, to warm through. Serve.

Serves 4.

SEAFOOD RISOTTO

1 tablespoon olive oil
6 spring onions, chopped
1 clove garlic, crushed
225 g (8 oz/1 cup) risotto rice
½ teaspoon turmeric
500 ml (18 fl oz/2¼ cups) fish stock
55 ml (2 fl oz/¼ cup) dry white wine
4 tomatoes, chopped
450 g (1 lb) mixed cooked seafood
12 tiger prawns
175 g (6 oz) frozen peas
salt and freshly ground black pepper
4 tablespoons chopped fresh parsley

Heat the oil in a large flameproof casserole. Add the spring onions and garlic and cook, stirring, for 3 minutes, until soft. Cover and cook over a gentle heat for 2 minutes. Add the rice and turmeric and cook, stirring, for 1 minute. Add half the stock, the wine and the tomatoes to the casserole. Bring to the boil, cover and simmer for 10 minutes.

Add the remaining stock, bring back to the boil, cover and cook for 15 minutes, until the rice has absorbed most of the liquid. Stir in the seafood, prawns, peas and salt and pepper. Cook gently, stirring occasionally, for 10 minutes. Stir in the parsley and serve.

Serves 4.

- MACKEREL WITH SOUR CREAM -

4 x 115 g (4 oz) mackerel fillets, skinned
1 leek, thinly sliced
200 g (7 oz) can chopped tomatoes
1 tablespoon chopped fresh dill
½ teaspoon mild paprika
juice of ½ lemon
salt
150 ml (5 fl oz/⅔ cup) thick sour cream
dill sprigs, to garnish

Preheat oven to 200C (400F/Gas 6). Place the
mackerel fillets in a shallow ovenproof dish.

In a large bowl, mix together the leek,
tomatoes, dill, paprika and lemon juice and
pour over the mackerel. Season with salt.

Cover with a lid or piece of foil and cook in
the oven for 50 minutes, until the fish is
cooked through. Drizzle over the sour cream,
garnish with dill sprigs and serve.

Serves 4.

SEAFOOD LASAGNE

2 tablespoons olive oil
1 leek, thinly sliced
225 g (8 oz) mushrooms, thinly sliced
225 g (8 oz) haddock fillet, skinned and cubed
115 g (4 oz) cooked, peeled prawns
300 g (10 oz) cod fillet, skinned and cubed
2 tablespoons lemon juice
salt and freshly ground black pepper
4 eggs, beaten
55 g (2 oz/½ cup) freshly grated Parmesan cheese
500 ml (18 fl oz/2¼ cups) Greek yogurt
6 sheets fresh lasagne
225 g (8 oz) mozzarella cheese, sliced

Heat the oil in a large flameproof dish and add the leek and mushrooms.

Cook gently for 10 minutes, stirring occasionally, until soft. Add the haddock, prawns, cod, lemon juice and salt and pepper and cook, stirring, for 5 minutes. Preheat oven to 180C (350F/Gas 4). Mix together the eggs, Parmesan cheese and yogurt. Stir into the fish mixture. Remove two-thirds of the fish mixture from the dish.

Cover the fish mixture in the dish with two sheets of lasagne. Cover them with half the remaining mixture then two more sheets of lasagne. Reserve a ladleful of the liquid from the fish mixture and spread the remaining mixture over the lasagne. Cover with two sheets of lasagne and pour the reserved liquid over the top. Cover with the cheese and bake for 40-50 minutes, until the topping is golden and the pasta is tender. Serve.

Serves 6-8.

——HADDOCK & SALMON PIE——

55 g (2 oz/¼ cup) butter
55 g (2 oz/½ cup) plain flour
300 ml (10 fl oz/1¼ cups) milk
300 ml (10 fl oz/1¼ cups) fish stock
12 shallots
450 g (1 lb) potatoes, diced
2 cloves garlic, crushed
2 tablespoons olive oil
1 tablespoon double (thick) cream
salt and freshly ground black pepper
2 tablespoons wholegrain mustard
4 tablespoons chopped fresh parsley
450 g (1 lb) salmon fillet, skinned and cubed
225 g (8 oz) smoked haddock, skinned and cubed
12 small button mushrooms
1 egg, beaten

Melt the butter in a flameproof casserole, add the flour and cook over a gentle heat, stirring, for 2 minutes. Gradually stir in the milk and fish stock, then add the shallots. Bring to the boil and simmer for 30 minutes. Meanwhile, cook the potatoes and garlic in boiling salted water for 20 minutes, until the potatoes are tender. Drain. Mash the potatoes and garlic and stir in the olive oil, cream and salt and pepper. Set aside. Preheat oven to 200C (400F/Gas 6).

Season the shallot sauce with salt and pepper and add the mustard and parsley. Add the salmon, haddock and button mushrooms and simmer gently for 10 minutes. Pipe or spoon the potato on top of the fish mixture and bake for 10 minutes. Take out of the oven and brush with a little beaten egg. Return to the oven and bake for 20 minutes, until the potato is golden. Serve.

Serves 4-6.

——— HALIBUT WITH ORANGE ———

55 g (2 oz/½ cup) plain flour
½ teaspoon freshly grated nutmeg
4 x 175 g (6 oz) halibut steaks
25 g (1 oz/ 2 tablespoons) butter
6 spring onions, sliced
175 ml (6 fl oz/¾ cup) fresh orange juice
1 tablespoon Worcestershire sauce
juice of ½ lemon
salt and freshly ground black pepper

Mix together the flour and nutmeg and use
to coat the halibut.

Heat the butter in a shallow ovenproof dish.
Add the spring onions and cook, stirring
occasionally, for 3 minutes, until soft. Add
the halibut and cook gently for 5-6 minutes
on each side until just cooked. Remove from
the pan with a fish slice and keep warm.

Add the orange juice, Worcestershire sauce,
lemon juice and salt and pepper to the dish
and boil rapidly until reduced and thickened.
Pour over the fish and serve.

Serves 4.

——PASTA WITH TUNA SAUCE——

225 g (8 oz) pasta twists
200 g (7 oz) can tuna in brine, drained
200 g (7 oz) can sweetcorn, drained
1 green pepper (capsicum), diced
4 spring onions, cut into 2.5 cm (1 inch) lengths
300 g (10 oz) can condensed mushroom soup mixed
    with ½ can water
salt and freshly ground black pepper
flat-leaf parsley sprigs, to garnish

Add the pasta twists to a large flameproof casserole of boiling salted water and cook for 10 minutes, or according to packet instructions, until just tender.

Drain the pasta and return to the casserole. Add the tuna, sweetcorn, pepper (capsicum) and spring onions and stir to combine.

Stir the soup into the casserole. Cook gently, stirring occasionally, for 20 minutes. Season with salt and pepper. Garnish with flat-leaf parsley and serve.

Serves 4.

——— TUNA-STUFFED PEPPERS ———

4 large green peppers (capsicum)
175 g (6 oz/¾ cup) long grain rice, cooked
200 g (7 oz) can tuna in brine, drained and flaked
1 small onion, grated
200 g (7 oz) can sweetcorn, drained
55 g (2 oz) mushrooms, finely chopped
1 teaspoon paprika
salt and freshly ground black pepper
55 g (2 oz/½ cup) grated Cheddar cheese
4 slices tomato

Trim the base of each pepper (capsicum) so it will stand. Combine the rice, tuna, onion, sweetcorn, mushrooms, paprika and salt and pepper. Pack into the peppers (capsicum).

Preheat oven to 180C (350F/Gas 4). Place the peppers (capsicum) in a shallow ovenproof dish. Pour 850 ml (30 fl oz/3¾ cups) water into the dish and bake for 30 minutes.

Remove from the oven and increase the temperature to 200C (400F/Gas 6). Sprinkle the peppers (capsicum) with cheese. Top each one with a slice of tomato and return to the oven for 10 minutes. Serve.

Serves 4.

— PASTA WITH SALMON TROUT —

1 tablespoon olive oil
225 g (8 oz) salmon trout fillets, skinned and cubed
225 g (8 oz) small broccoli flowerets
300 g (10 oz) tagliatelle
150 ml (5 fl oz/⅔ cup) single (light) cream
1 tablespoon chopped fresh dill
salt and freshly ground black pepper
25 g (1 oz/¼ cup) toasted flaked almonds

Heat the oil in a flameproof casserole. Add the salmon and broccoli and cook, stirring occasionally, for 10-15 minutes, until the fish is just cooked and the broccoli is tender.

Meanwhile, cook the tagliatelle in boiling salted water for 8-10 minutes, or according to packet instructions, until just tender. Drain and stir in to the casserole.

Stir in the single (light) cream and dill and season with salt and pepper. Sprinkle with toasted almonds and serve.

Serves 4.

——CANTONESE PRAWNS——

1 tablespoon olive oil
1 onion, sliced
2 tablespoons Cantonese spice mixture
450 g (1 lb) cooked, peeled tiger prawns
1 red pepper (capsicum), sliced
225 g (8 oz) canned sliced water chestnuts, drained
175 g (6 oz) mange tout (snow peas)
flat-leaf parsley, to garnish

Heat the oil in a flameproof casserole. Add the onion and cook, stirring occasionally, for 5 minutes, until soft. Add the Cantonese spice and cook, stirring, for 1 minute. Add the prawns and cook for 2-3 minutes.

Stir in the pepper (capsicum), water chestnuts and mange tout (snow peas). Cover and cook for 2-3 minutes. Garnish with flat-leaf parsley and serve.

Serves 2-3.

Note: Cantonese spice is a ready-mixed blend available in large supermarkets.

—SMOKED MACKEREL GRATIN—

450 g (1 lb) peppered smoked mackerel, skinned
   and flaked
4 tablespoons chopped fresh parsley
500 ml (18 fl oz/2¼ cups) fromage frais
6 teaspoons horseradish sauce
6-8 drops Tabasco sauce
1 red onion, finely chopped
2 tablespoons grated Parmesan cheese
175 g (6 oz/3 cups) fresh wholemeal breadcrumbs
25 g (1 oz) sunflower seeds

Preheat oven to 200C (400F/Gas 6). Mix
together the mackerel, parsley, fromage frais,
horseradish sauce, Tabasco sauce and onion.

Spread the mackerel mixture into a shallow
ovenproof dish. Mix together the Parmesan
cheese, breadcrumbs and sunflower seeds.

Scatter over the mackerel mixture and bake
for 20 minutes, until golden. Serve.

Serves 4-6.

—COD & VEGETABLE PARCELS—

vegetable oil, for greasing
4 x 175 g (6 oz) cod steaks
225 g (8 oz) frozen mixed vegetables
6 spring onions, sliced
2 tablespoons ginger wine
2 teaspoons soy sauce
1 cm (½ in) piece fresh root ginger, peeled and
   thinly sliced
lemon slices, to serve

Preheat oven to 200C (400F/Gas 6). Cut four
large squares of foil and lightly oil. Place a
cod steak on each one. Arrange the frozen
vegetables and spring onions on top.

Mix together the ginger wine and soy sauce
and spoon over the cod steaks. Put the sliced
ginger on top.

Bring the foil up over the steaks and fold the
edges together, to seal. Put the parcels in an
ovenproof dish and bake for 20-25 minutes.
Remove the fish and vegetables from the
parcels and serve with lemon slices.

Serves 4.

── TROUT WITH VEGETABLES ──

2 x 400 g (14 oz) cans chopped tomatoes
1 leek, finely sliced
12 basil leaves, torn
2 teaspoons chopped fresh oregano
3 sticks celery, diced
2 courgettes (zucchini), diced
175 ml (6 fl oz/¾ cup) red wine
2 tablespoons red wine vinegar
salt and freshly ground black pepper
4 trout, cleaned
4 basil sprigs
8 oregano sprigs

Put the tomatoes, leek, torn basil, chopped oregano, celery, courgettes (zucchini), wine and vinegar in a shallow flameproof dish.

Bring to the boil, cover with a lid or piece of foil and simmer for 10 minutes. Season with salt and pepper. Stuff the trout cavities with the basil sprigs and half the oregano sprigs.

Place the trout on top of the vegetable mixture. Cover again and simmer gently for 20-25 minutes, until the trout is cooked through. Garnish with the remaining oregano sprigs and serve.

Serves 4.

– POUSSINS WITH WATERCRESS –

4 small oven-ready poussins
watercress sprigs, to garnish
STUFFING:
115 g (4 oz/2 cups) fresh wholemeal breadcrumbs
55 g (2 oz) ready-to-eat dried apricots, chopped
1 small bunch watercress, chopped
55 g (2 oz/½ cup) hazelnuts, chopped
salt and freshly ground black pepper
1 egg yolk
WATERCRESS SAUCE:
1 onion, finely chopped
1 bunch watercress, chopped
115 ml (4 fl oz/½ cup) dry white wine
1 tablespoon chopped fresh tarragon
1 teaspoon lemon juice
55 ml (2 fl oz/¼ cup) Greek yogurt

Preheat oven to 200C (400F/Gas 6). To make the stuffing, mix together the breadcrumbs, apricots, watercress, hazelnuts and salt and pepper. Bind together with the egg yolk. Use to stuff the cavity of each poussin. Place the poussins in a shallow flameproof dish and roast for 50-60 minutes, until cooked through. To test, pierce the thigh with a skewer: if the juices run clear the poussins are cooked. Remove the poussins from the dish and keep warm.

To make the watercress sauce, add the onion to the cooking juices in the dish and cook gently, stirring occasionally, for 5 minutes, until soft. Add the chopped watercress and stir well. Add the white wine, tarragon and lemon juice and heat gently. Stir in the Greek yogurt and season with salt and pepper. Heat gently to warm through. Pour the sauce on to warmed serving plates and place the poussins on top. Garnish with watercress and serve.

Serves 4.

—CHILLI CHICKEN WITH RICE—

4 chicken joints
salt and freshly ground black pepper
150 ml (5 fl oz/⅔ cup) chicken stock
150 ml (5 fl oz/⅔ cup) dry white wine
1 teaspoon chilli sauce
225 g (8 oz/1 cup) basmati rice
1 onion, chopped
1 yellow pepper (capsicum), chopped
1 fresh green chilli, cored, seeded and chopped
400 g (14 oz) can chopped tomatoes
flat-leaf parsley sprigs, to garnish

Preheat oven to 220C (425F/Gas 7). Place the chicken portions in a large flameproof casserole. Season with salt and pepper.

Cook in the oven for 20 minutes. Remove the chicken from the casserole and keep warm. Lower the oven temperature to 190C (375F/Gas 5). Add the stock, white wine, chilli sauce and 115 ml (4 fl oz/½ cup) boiling water to the casserole. Add the rice, onion and yellow pepper (capsicum). Stir in the chopped green chilli and tomatoes.

Place the chicken on top of the rice mixture. Cover and bake for 45 minutes, until the rice is tender and the liquid has been absorbed. Garnish with flat-leaf parsley and serve.

Serves 4.

——————— SPICY CHICKEN ———————

2 cloves garlic, crushed
1 cm (½ in) piece fresh root ginger, peeled and very
    thinly sliced
1 tablespoon soy sauce
½ teaspoon five-spice powder
1.35 kg (3 lb) chicken, cut into 8 pieces
2 tablespoons olive oil
2 onions, thinly sliced
1 red pepper (capsicum), thinly sliced
8 plum tomatoes, peeled, quartered and seeded
2 tablespoons chopped fresh coriander

In a large bowl, mix together the garlic, ginger, soy sauce and five-spice powder. Add the chicken and turn to coat.

Cover and leave to marinate for 2 hours. Preheat oven to 180C (350F/Gas 4). Heat the oil in a large flameproof casserole. Add the onions and pepper (capsicum), cover and cook gently for 10-15 minutes, until soft but not coloured. Add the tomatoes.

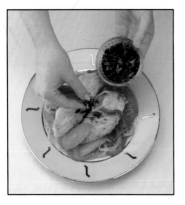

Add the chicken and marinade, cover and cook in the oven for 25-30 minutes, until the chicken is cooked through. Sprinkle with coriander and serve.

Serves 4.

CHICKEN CRUMBLE

1 tablespoon olive oil
450 g (1 lb) skinless, boneless chicken breast, cubed
1 leek, sliced
225 g (8 oz) mushrooms, thinly sliced
115 g (4 oz) frozen peas
450 ml (16 fl oz/2 cups) Greek yogurt
2 teaspoons wholegrain mustard
salt and freshly ground black pepper
55 g (2 oz/⅔ cup) rolled oats
55 g (2 oz/½ cup) wholemeal flour
55 g (2 oz/¼ cup) butter
55 g (2 oz/1 cup) fresh wholemeal breadcrumbs
1 tablespoon grated Parmesan cheese
2 teaspoons dried thyme
1 tablespoon sesame seeds
thyme sprigs, to garnish

Heat the oil in a large flameproof casserole. Add the chicken cubes and cook, stirring, until golden on all sides. Add the leek and cook, stirring occasionally, for 10 minutes, until the leek is soft. Preheat oven to 200C (400F/Gas 6). Add the mushrooms and peas to the casserole and cook for 3-5 minutes, until the peas have thawed. Remove from the heat and stir in the Greek yogurt, mustard and salt and pepper.

Put the oats and flour in a bowl and rub in the butter until the mixture resembles breadcrumbs. Stir in the breadcrumbs, Parmesan cheese, thyme and sesame seeds. Sprinkle the mixture evenly over the top of the chicken and bake for 40-45 minutes, until the topping is golden brown. Garnish with thyme sprigs and serve.

Serves 4.

— GARLIC ROASTED CHICKEN —

2 tablespoons olive oil
6 cloves garlic, thinly sliced
8 chicken thighs
115 g (4 oz) fennel, cut into wide strips
1 carrot, cut into wide strips
1 parsnip, cut into wide strips
1 large potato, diced
1 red pepper (capsicum), diced
1 green pepper (capsicum), diced

Preheat oven to 220C (425F/Gas 7). Heat the oil in a shallow flameproof dish. Add the garlic and cook for 2-3 minutes. Add the chicken and vegetables and turn to coat.

Roast for 55-60 minutes, until the chicken is cooked through and golden. Serve.

Serves 4.

—FLEMISH BRAISED CHICKEN—

55 g (2 oz/¼ cup) butter
1.8 kg (4 lb) chicken
450 g (1 lb) leeks, sliced
225 g (8 oz) carrots, sliced
½ head celery, chopped
115 g (4 oz) button mushrooms, halved
550 ml (20 fl oz/2½ cups) chicken stock
2 bay leaves
12 small new potatoes
250 ml (9 fl oz/1 cup) dry white wine
70 ml (2½ fl oz/⅓ cup) double (thick) cream
2 egg yolks
flat-leaf parsley sprigs and chopped parsley, to garnish

Melt the butter in a flameproof casserole. Add the chicken and brown all over.

Remove from the casserole. Preheat oven to 200C (400F/Gas 6). Add the leeks, carrots, celery and mushrooms to the casserole and stir well. Cover and cook for 5-10 minutes, until soft. Add the stock and bay leaves. Bring to the boil and add the chicken. Cover and cook in the oven for 30 minutes. Add the potatoes and cook for 30 minutes. Lift out the chicken and remove the vegetables with a slotted spoon. Keep warm.

Add the wine to the casserole and bring to the boil. Reduce to a simmer. In a large bowl, mix together the cream and the egg yolks. Pour the simmering stock on to the cream mixture, stirring constantly. Return to the casserole and heat gently. Do not boil. Return the vegetables to the casserole. Carve the chicken, garnish with flat-leaf parsley sprigs and chopped parsley and serve with the vegetables and sauce.

Serves 6.

THAI CHICKEN

2 teaspoons olive oil
1 fresh red chilli, cored, seeded and finely chopped
2.5 cm (1 in) piece fresh root ginger, peeled and
   grated
1 teaspoon lemon grass paste
225 g (8 oz) chanterelle mushrooms
1-2 teaspoons Thai red curry paste
250 ml (9 fl oz/1 cup) coconut milk
1 tablespoon light soy sauce
350 g (12 oz) skinless, boneless chicken breast, cubed
coriander sprigs and chopped coriander, to garnish

Heat the oil in a flameproof casserole. Add
the chilli, ginger, lemon grass paste and
mushrooms and stir-fry for 2-3 minutes.

Add the curry paste and stir-fry for 1 minute.
Add the coconut milk and soy sauce and
bring to the boil.

Add the chicken and simmer for 10 minutes,
until the chicken is tender and cooked
through. Garnish with coriander sprigs and
chopped coriander and serve.

Serves 4.

Note: If lemon grass paste is not available,
replace it with 1 teaspoon chopped fresh
lemon grass, or ½ teaspoon dried.

─────────── STIR-FRIED DUCK ───────────

4 x 115 g (4 oz) boneless duck breasts
2 tablespoons vegetable oil
1 clove garlic, crushed
2.5 cm (1 in) piece fresh root ginger, peeled and
　grated
4 tablespoons soy sauce
225 g (8 oz) carrots, cut into matchsticks
225 g (8 oz) mange tout (snow peas)
3 sticks celery, cut into matchsticks
300 g (10 oz) bean sprouts
1 teaspoon cornflour

Remove the skin and excess fat from the
duck breasts and cut the flesh into strips.

Heat the oil and garlic in a large flameproof
casserole. Add the duck, ginger and soy
sauce and stir-fry for 3-4 minutes. Add the
carrots, mange tout (snow peas) and celery
and stir-fry for 5 minutes. Add the bean
sprouts and stir-fry for 1 minute.

Blend the cornflour with 2 tablespoons of
water and add to the casserole. Cook,
stirring, for 1-2 minutes, until the juices have
thickened. Serve.

Serves 4.

-DUCK WITH APPLES & PRUNES-

1 tablespoon olive oil
4 x 115 g (4 oz) boneless duck breasts
2 cooking apples, peeled, cored and sliced
225 g (8 oz) ready-to-eat prunes
550 ml (20 fl oz/2 ½ cups) dry cider
salt and freshly ground black pepper

Preheat oven to 200C (400F/Gas 6). Heat the oil in a shallow flameproof dish, add the duck and cook for 3-4 minutes on each side, until browned.

Cover with the apple slices and prunes. Pour the cider over the duck and season with salt and pepper. Bring to the boil, cover with a lid or piece of foil and cook in the oven for 55-60 minutes, until the duck is cooked through. Remove the duck from the dish with a slotted spoon, leaving behind the apples and prunes, and keep warm.

Bring the cooking juices in the dish to the boil and boil for 5 minutes, until the liquid has reduced and thickened. Pour the sauce, apples and prunes over the duck and serve.

Serves 4.

GREEK MEATBALLS

450 g (1 lb) minced turkey
1 onion, finely chopped
1 clove garlic, crushed
1 tablespoon chopped fresh parsley
1 tablespoon chopped fresh mint
3 eggs, separated
55 g (2 oz/½ cup) cooked rice
salt and freshly ground black pepper
1 litre (35 fl oz/4½ cups) chicken stock
juice of 1 lemon
225 g (8 oz) frozen peas
mint sprigs, to garnish

Mix together the turkey, onion, garlic, herbs, egg yolks, rice and salt and pepper. Divide the mixture into 24 balls.

Leave the mixture to rest for 20 minutes. Place the meatballs in a single layer in a large flameproof casserole. Cover with the chicken stock. Bring to the boil and simmer gently for 20 minutes, turning regularly to ensure even cooking. Remove the meatballs with a slotted spoon and keep warm. Boil the stock until reduced by two-thirds.

Beat the egg whites with the lemon juice until frothy. Add to the hot stock in the casserole. Stir in the peas and return the meatballs to the casserole. Heat gently to warm through. Garnish with mint sprigs and serve.

Serves 4.

TURKEY KORMA

1 teaspoon turmeric
1 teaspoon ground cumin
1 teaspoon ground coriander
½ teaspoon ground ginger
150 ml (5 fl oz/⅔ cup) natural yogurt
2 teaspoons lemon juice
115 ml (4 fl oz/½ cup) coconut milk
115 ml (4 fl oz/½ cup) chicken stock
85 g (3 oz) unsweetened desiccated coconut
salt and freshly ground black pepper
450 g (1 lb) cooked turkey meat, cubed
coriander sprigs, to garnish

Preheat oven to 190C (375F/Gas 5). Dry-fry the turmeric, cumin, coriander and ginger in a flameproof casserole for 2-3 minutes.

Add the yogurt, lemon juice, coconut milk, stock, desiccated coconut and salt and pepper and mix well. Stir in the turkey.

Bring to the boil, cover and cook in the oven for 30-40 minutes. Garnish with coriander sprigs and serve.

Serves 4.

— GINGER TURKEY & CABBAGE —

300 ml (10 fl oz/1 ¼ cups) red wine
2 tablespoons red wine vinegar
115 g (4 oz) sultanas
225 g (8 oz) ready-to-eat dried apricots, halved
2.5 cm (1 in) piece fresh root ginger, peeled and
    grated
2 cloves garlic, crushed
salt and freshly ground black pepper
4 x 175 g (6 oz) turkey breast fillets
½ red cabbage, shredded
flat-leaf parsley sprigs, to garnish

In a large bowl, mix together the red wine,
vinegar, sultanas, apricots, ginger, garlic and
salt and pepper. Add the turkey.

Cover and marinate for at least 2 hours,
preferably overnight. Preheat oven to 200C
(400F/Gas 6). Arrange the red cabbage in a
shallow ovenproof dish. Remove the turkey
from the marinade and mix the marinade
with the cabbage. Place the turkey on top.

Cook in the oven for 45-50 minutes, until the
turkey is tender and cooked through.
Garnish with flat-leaf parsley and serve.

Serves 4.

TURKEY MILANESE

1 egg, beaten
115 g (4 oz/2 cups) fresh white breadcrumbs
grated rind and juice of 1 lemon
salt and freshly ground black pepper
4 x 115 g (4 oz) turkey breast fillets, flattened
25 g (1 oz/2 tablespoons) butter
2 tablespoons olive oil
350 g (12 oz) courgettes (zucchini), sliced
2 teaspoons chopped fresh tarragon
lemon wedges, to serve

Place the egg on a large plate. Mix together the breadcrumbs, lemon rind and salt and pepper and put on a large plate. Dip the turkey in the egg and then the breadcrumbs.

Preheat oven to 200C (400F/Gas 6). Heat the butter and oil in a shallow flameproof dish. Add the turkey and cook for 3 minutes on each side, until crisp and golden. Add the courgettes (zucchini) and tarragon.

Sprinkle with the lemon juice and season with pepper. Cover and cook in the oven for 35-40 minutes. Serve with lemon wedges.

Serves 4.

— TURKEY WITH CHESTNUTS —

4 x 175 g (6 oz) turkey breast fillets
115 g (4 oz) streaky bacon, chopped
55 ml (2 fl oz/¼ cup) olive oil
2 tablespoons chopped fresh parsley
1 teaspoon caster sugar
1 tablespoon balsamic vinegar
freshly ground black pepper
240 g (8½ oz) can chestnuts, roughly chopped
115 g (4 oz) cherry tomatoes, halved
flat-leaf parsley sprigs, to garnish

Put the turkey in a shallow flameproof dish
and scatter the bacon on top. Cook over a
medium heat for 15 minutes, turning once,
until golden and cooked through.

Remove the turkey and bacon with a slotted
spoon and keep warm. In a bowl, whisk
together the olive oil, parsley, sugar, balsamic
vinegar and pepper. Stir in the chestnuts and
cherry tomatoes.

Stir the chestnut mixture into the cooking
juices in the dish and cook, stirring, for 2
minutes. Divide the relish among warmed
serving plates and place the turkey breasts
and bacon on top. Garnish with flat-leaf
parsley and serve.

Serves 4.

— PHEASANT IN PARSLEY SAUCE —

55 g (2 oz/¼ cup) butter
2 pheasants
85 g (3 oz) fresh parsley
3 onions, thinly sliced
25 g (1 oz/¼ cup) plain flour
300 ml (10 fl oz/1¼ cups) chicken stock
150 ml (5 fl oz/⅔ cup) crème fraîche
salt and freshly ground black pepper
flat-leaf parsley sprigs, to garnish

Preheat oven to 180C (350F/Gas 4). Melt the butter in a large flameproof dish. Add the pheasants and cook until browned all over. Remove and keep warm.

Separate the thick parsley stalks from the leaves and tie the stalks together with string. Chop the leaves and set aside. Add the onions to the dish and cook, stirring occasionally, for 7 minutes, until soft and lightly coloured. Add the flour and cook, stirring, for 1 minute. Gradually add the chicken stock, stirring constantly until smooth. Bring to the boil and add the bundle of parsley stalks. Add the pheasants, cover and cook in the oven for 1 hour.

Remove the pheasants from the dish and keep warm. Remove and discard the parsley stalks. Add the chopped parsley and crème fraîche to the sauce and season with salt and pepper. Heat gently to warm through. Cut the pheasants in half with kitchen scissors. Garnish with flat-leaf parsley sprigs and serve with the parsley sauce.

Serves 4.

—RABBIT IN MUSTARD SAUCE—

55 g (2 oz/¼ cup) butter
8 rabbit portions
250 ml (9 fl oz/1 cup) dry white wine
115 g (4 oz) Dijon mustard
1 thyme sprig
salt and freshly ground black pepper
115 ml (4 fl oz/½ cup) Greek yogurt
chopped fresh flat-leaf parsley and thyme sprigs, to
  garnish

Melt the butter in a flameproof casserole.
Add the rabbit and cook for 5-10 minutes,
turning, until browned all over. Remove with
a slotted spoon.

Stir in the wine, mustard, thyme and salt and
pepper and bring to the boil. Return the
rabbit to the casserole, cover and simmer for
25 minutes. Remove the rabbit with a slotted
spoon and keep warm.

Boil the sauce until reduced by half. Remove
and discard the thyme sprig and stir in the
yogurt. Heat gently to warm through.
Garnish the rabbit with chopped parsley and
thyme sprigs, pour over the sauce and serve.

Serves 4.

—QUAIL IN A MASALA SAUCE—

8 quails
1 tablespoon melted butter
mint sprigs and salad leaves, to garnish
MARINADE:
300 ml (10 fl oz/1¼ cups) Greek yogurt
1 small onion, finely chopped
1 tablespoon finely chopped fresh mint leaves
1 tablespoon finely chopped fresh coriander leaves
1 clove garlic, crushed
2.5 cm (1 in) piece fresh root ginger, peeled and grated
1 tablespoon garam masala
juice of 1 lemon
1 teaspoon salt

Put the quails in a large dish. Mix together the marinade ingredients and pour over the quails.

Cover and marinate for at least 2 hours, preferably overnight. Preheat oven to 220C (425F/Gas 7). Remove the quails from the marinade, reserving the marinade. Thread the quails on to skewers and sit the skewers over an ovenproof dish.

Cook in the oven for 40 minutes, basting with the melted butter, until the quails are cooked through. Remove the quails and keep warm. Add the reserved marinade to the dish and stir to combine with the cooking juices. Bring to the boil, stirring. Garnish the quails with mint sprigs and salad leaves and serve with the masala sauce.

Serves 4.

—— PAN-FRIED GUINEA FOWL ——

1 tablespoon olive oil
2 guinea fowl
115 g (4 oz) streaky bacon, chopped
175 g (6 oz) button mushrooms
175 g (6 oz) shallots
2 tablespoons brandy
250 ml (9 fl oz/1 cup) red wine
550 ml (20 fl oz/2½ cups) chicken stock
3 tablespoons redcurrant jelly
salt and freshly ground black pepper
marjoram sprigs, to garnish

Preheat oven to 180C (350F/Gas 4). Heat the oil in an ovenproof dish. Add the guinea fowl and brown all over.

Cover and cook in the oven for 35-40 minutes. Remove and keep warm. Add the bacon, mushrooms and shallots to the dish and cook, stirring, for 4-5 minutes, until golden brown. Remove with a slotted spoon and keep warm. Add the brandy, wine, stock and redcurrant jelly to the cooking juices and stir well. Bring to the boil, stirring, and boil for 20-25 minutes, stirring occasionally, until the sauce is reduced and thickened.

Return the guinea fowl, bacon, mushrooms and shallots to the casserole and season well. Bring to the boil and simmer for 4-5 minutes to warm through. Cut the guinea fowl in half with kitchen scissors or a sharp knife. Garnish with marjoram sprigs and serve.

Serves 4.

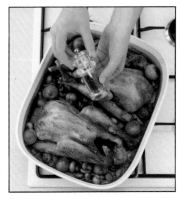

BOBOTIE

250 ml (9 fl oz/1 cup) milk
1 thick slice white bread
1 tablespoon olive oil
1 large onion, chopped
1 kg (2¼ lb) minced beef
2 teaspoons apricot jam
55 ml (2 fl oz/¼ cup) lemon juice
85 g (3 oz) seedless raisins
10 ready-to-eat dried apricots
2 tablespoons mild curry powder
12 blanched almonds, roughly chopped
1 teaspoon salt
freshly ground black pepper
6 bay leaves
2 eggs

Preheat oven to 180C (350F/Gas 4). Put half the milk in a shallow dish, add the bread and leave to soak for 5 minutes. Heat the oil in a flameproof casserole. Add the onion and cook, stirring occasionally, for 5 minutes, until soft. Squeeze the milk from the bread and add the bread to the casserole with all the remaining ingredients except the eggs and remaining milk. Mix well then level the surface. Bake for 30 minutes.

Beat together the remaining milk and eggs and pour over the meat. Return to the oven and bake for 20-25 minutes, until the custard has set.

Serves 6-8.

Note: This dish is particularly good served with a fruity chutney.

POT ROAST OF BRISKET

1.35 kg (3 lb) brisket of beef
2 leeks, thickly sliced
1 bay leaf
2 parsley stalks
1 celery leaf
450 g (1 lb) carrots, thickly sliced
450 g (1 lb) sweet potatoes, cut into chunks
4 tablespoons cider vinegar
225 g (8 oz) white cabbage, thickly shredded
salt and freshly ground black pepper

Heat a large flameproof casserole, add the brisket and cook, turning, for 3-4 minutes, until browned all over.

Remove from the casserole. Add the leeks and mix into the cooking juices. With a piece of string, tie together the bay leaf, parsley stalks and celery leaf and add to the casserole with the carrots and sweet potatoes. Stir well. Add the vinegar and 115 ml (4 fl oz/½ cup) water. Put the meat on top.

Cover and cook very gently for 2½ hours. Remove the beef from the casserole and keep warm. Remove the vegetables with a slotted spoon and keep warm. Bring the sauce to the boil and add the white cabbage. Season and simmer for 5 minutes. Carve the beef and serve with the vegetables.

Serves 6-8.

-MEATBALLS IN TOMATO SAUCE-

55 ml (2 fl oz/¼ cup) milk
1 egg, beaten
½ teaspoon freshly grated nutmeg
55 g (2 oz) white bread
2 onions, finely chopped
2 cloves garlic, crushed
1 teaspoon dried thyme
2 tablespoons chopped fresh parsley
450 g (1 lb) minced beef
1 tablespoon olive oil
400 g (14 oz) can chopped tomatoes
2 tablespoons tomato purée (paste)
salt and freshly ground black pepper
basil leaves, to garnish

In a shallow dish, mix together the milk, egg
and nutmeg. Add the bread and leave to soak
for 5 minutes. In a bowl, mix half the onions
and garlic with the thyme, parsley and
minced beef. Squeeze the liquid from the
bread and add the bread to the beef mixture.
Mix well and shape into 30 balls. Heat the oil
in a flameproof casserole. Add the meatballs
in batches and cook, turning, for about
8 minutes, until browned all over. Remove
with a slotted spoon, drain on kitchen paper
and keep warm.

Put the remaining onion and garlic in the
casserole with the chopped tomatoes, tomato
purée (paste) and salt and pepper. Bring to
the boil and cook over a medium heat,
stirring constantly, until reduced and
thickened. Add the meatballs and heat gently
to warm through. Garnish and serve.

Serves 4.

— BEEF GOULASH WITH CHILLI —

2 tablespoons olive oil
1 onion, sliced
1 clove garlic, crushed
2 teaspoons paprika
700 g (1½ lb) lean stewing beef, cubed
pinch of caraway seeds
2 bay leaves
1 tablespoon balsamic vinegar
450 ml (16 fl oz/2 cups) beef stock
salt and freshly ground black pepper
700 g (1½ lb) potatoes, diced
2 green peppers (capsicum), sliced
1 fresh green chilli, cored, seeded and sliced
400 g (14 oz) can chopped tomatoes
2 tablespoons tomato purée (paste)

Heat the oil in a flameproof casserole. Add the onion, garlic and paprika and cook, stirring, for 2 minutes. Add the beef and cook for 3-4 minutes, until the onion is soft and the beef has browned. Add the caraway seeds, bay leaves, vinegar and half the stock. Season with salt and pepper and bring to the boil. Cover and simmer for 1 hour.

Stir in the remaining stock, potatoes, peppers (capsicum), chilli, tomatoes and tomato purée (paste). Bring to the boil, cover and simmer for 30-40 minutes, until the meat and vegetables are tender.

Serves 4.

—BELGIAN HOTCHPOTCH—

225 g (8 oz) brisket of beef, cubed
225 g (8 oz) shoulder of lamb, cubed
85 g (3 oz) belly pork, cubed
500 ml (18 fl oz/2¼ cups) chicken stock
2 bay leaves
salt and freshly ground black pepper
115 g (4 oz) swede, diced
10 small onions
225 g (8 oz) Brussels sprouts
700 g (1½ lb) potatoes, diced
115 g (4 oz) carrots, diced
225 g (8 oz) pork chipolata sausages
150 ml (5 fl oz/⅔ cup) crème fraîche

Put the beef, lamb and pork in a flameproof casserole and pour in the stock.

Add 500 ml (18 fl oz/2¼ cups) water, the bay leaves and 1 teaspoon salt. Bring to the boil, skimming any scum from the surface. Cover tightly and simmer for 2 hours. Add the vegetables and cook for 30 minutes, until the meat is tender. Remove the meat and vegetables from the casserole with a slotted spoon and keep warm. Put the sausages in the casserole and cook for 10 minutes. Remove with a slotted spoon and add to the meat and vegetables.

Bring the sauce to the boil and boil until reduced by one-third. Season with salt and pepper, stir in the crème fraîche and heat gently to warm through. Pour the sauce over the meat and vegetables and serve.

Serves 4-6.

— CHORIZO & BEAN CASSEROLE —

1 tablespoon olive oil
1 onion, thinly sliced
10 chorizo sausages, cut into chunks
400 g (14 oz) can pinto beans, drained
400 g (14 oz) can canellini beans, drained
400 g (14 oz) can chopped tomatoes
250 ml (9 fl oz/1 cup) vegetable stock
salt and freshly ground black pepper
3 potatoes, thinly sliced

Preheat oven to 200C (400F/Gas 6). Heat the oil in a flameproof casserole. Add the onion and cook, stirring occasionally, for 5 minutes, until soft. Add the chorizo sausages and cook for 4-5 minutes.

Add the beans, tomatoes, stock and salt and pepper and bring to the boil. Remove from the heat and arrange the sliced potatoes on top. Bake for 40-45 minutes, until the potatoes are tender and golden brown. Serve.

Serves 4.

—CHILLI BEEF WITH NACHOS—

1 tablespoon olive oil
1 onion, chopped
1 clove garlic, crushed
450 g (1 lb) minced beef
400 g (14 oz) can red kidney beans, drained
1 green pepper (capsicum), chopped
2 tablespoons tomato purée (paste)
2 teaspoons chilli powder
150 g (5 oz) tortilla chips
115 g (4 oz/1 cup) grated mozzarella cheese
1-2 teaspoons paprika

Heat the oil in a flameproof casserole. Add the onion and garlic and cook, stirring occasionally, for 5 minutes, until soft. Add the mince and cook for 6-8 minutes, until brown. Stir in the kidney beans, green peppers (capsicum), tomato purée (paste), chilli powder and 150 ml (5 fl oz/²⁄₃ cup) water. Cover and simmer for 10-15 minutes. Preheat oven to 200C (400F/Gas 6).

Uncover and cook for 5 minutes, until the sauce is reduced and thickened. Arrange the tortilla chips over the top, sprinkle with mozzarella cheese and paprika and cook in the oven for 20 minutes until the cheese is melted and golden. Serve.

Serves 4.

VENISON RAGOÛT

1 tablespoon plain flour
salt and freshly ground black pepper
900 g (2 lb) stewing venison, cubed
1 tablespoon olive oil
1 clove garlic, chopped
300 ml (10 fl oz/1¼ cups) beef stock
1 tablespoon balsamic vinegar
8 juniper berries
8 black peppercorns
4 cloves
400 g (14 oz) can chopped tomatoes
225 g (8 oz) baby carrots, trimmed
115 g (4 oz) button mushrooms
1 tablespoon chopped fresh parsley

Preheat oven to 180C (350F/Gas 4). Season the flour with salt and pepper and use to coat the venison. Heat the oil in a large flameproof casserole. Add the venison, the remaining seasoned flour and garlic and cook, stirring, for 4-5 minutes.

Add the stock, vinegar, juniper berries, peppercorns, cloves, tomatoes and carrots. Bring to the boil, cover and cook in the oven for 1 hour. Add the mushrooms and cook for 15 minutes. Sprinkle with chopped parsley and serve.

Serves 6-8.

— CURRIED LAMB WITH RAITA —

3 tablespoons olive oil
2 onions, finely chopped
1 cm (½ in) piece fresh root ginger, peeled and grated
3 cloves garlic, crushed
1 teaspoon chilli powder
1 ½ teaspoons turmeric
1 ½ teaspoons ground coriander
½ teaspoon each ground cumin and garam masala
450 g (1 lb) lamb fillet, cubed
115 ml (4 fl oz/½ cup) natural yogurt
salt and freshly ground black pepper
mint sprigs, to garnish
RAITA:
300 ml (10 fl oz/1¼ cups) natural yogurt
175 g (6 oz) cucumber, diced
1 tablespoon chopped fresh mint

Heat the oil in a flameproof casserole. Add the onions and cook, stirring occasionally, for 5 minutes, until soft. Add the ginger, garlic, chilli powder, turmeric, coriander, cumin and garam masala and cook, stirring, for 2 minutes. Add the lamb and cook, stirring, for 2 minutes, until browned.

Add the yogurt, 115 ml (4 fl oz/½ cup) water and salt and pepper and stir well. Bring to the boil and simmer gently for 45 minutes. Meanwhile, make the raita. Mix together the yogurt, cucumber and chopped mint. Season with salt and pepper. Chill until required. Garnish the lamb with mint sprigs and serve with the raita.

Serves 4.

HARVEST CASSEROLE

2 tablespoons olive oil
4 spare rib pork chops
1 large onion, sliced
2 leeks, chopped
1 clove garlic, crushed
225 g (8 oz) parsnips, cut into chunks
225 g (8 oz) carrots, cut into chunks
1 teaspoon dried sage
2 tablespoons plain flour
300 ml (10 fl oz/1¼ cups) beef stock
300 ml (10 fl oz/1¼ cups) apple juice
salt and freshly ground black pepper
2 small eating apples
175 g (6 oz/1½ cups) self-raising flour
85 g (3 oz) shredded suet
1 teaspoon mixed dried herbs

Preheat oven to 160C (325F/Gas 3). Heat the oil in a large flameproof casserole. Add the chops and cook for 2-3 minutes on each side until browned. Remove from the casserole and drain on kitchen paper. Add the onion, leeks and garlic and cook, stirring occasionally, for 5 minutes, until soft. Add the parsnips, carrots and sage and cook for 2 minutes. Add the plain flour and cook, stirring, for 1 minute. Gradually stir in the stock and apple juice. Season with salt and pepper and bring to the boil.

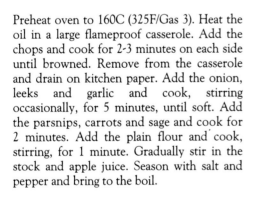

Replace the chops, cover and cook in the oven for 1¼ hours, or until the pork is tender. Meanwhile, core and roughly chop the apples and set aside. Mix together the self-raising flour, suet, herbs and salt and pepper. Add 175 ml (6 fl oz/¾ cup) water and bind to a firm dough. Divide the dough into eight small dumplings. Stir the apples into the casserole. Place the dumplings on top, return to the oven and cook, uncovered, for 20 minutes. Serve.

Serves 4.

─── STUFFED PORK SHOULDER ───

1.35 kg (3 lb) shoulder of pork, boned and skinned
450 g (1 lb) potatoes, cut into chunks
450 g (1 lb) swede, cut into chunks
450 g (1 lb) parsnips, cut into chunks
1 tablespoon olive oil
salt and freshly ground black pepper
1 tablespoon cornflour
500 ml (18 fl oz/2¼ cups) vegetable stock
1 tablespoon mango and lime chutney
sage leaves, to garnish
STUFFING:
175 g (6 oz) can corned beef, finely chopped
115 g (4 oz/2 cups) fresh white breadcrumbs
1 onion, finely chopped
1 teaspoon dried sage
1 tablespoon mango and lime chutney

Preheat oven to 180C (350F/Gas 4). Open out the shoulder of pork and flatten. To make the stuffing, mix together the corned beef, breadcrumbs, onion and sage. Add the chutney and bind the mixture together. Spread the stuffing along the centre of the inside of the pork. Roll the pork into a round shape and tie securely with string. Season with salt and pepper. Put in a flameproof dish, cover with a lid or piece of foil and cook in the oven for 2 hours, basting the meat every 45 minutes. Increase the oven temperature to 200C (400F/Gas 6).

Place the potatoes, swede and parsnips around the meat. Drizzle the vegetables with oil and season with salt and pepper. Cook, uncovered, for 45-55 minutes, turning the vegetables occasionally, until tender. Remove the meat and vegetables and keep warm. Add the cornflour and stir into the cooking juices. Gradually add the stock and bring to the boil, stirring. Add the chutney and simmer for 3-4 minutes. Slice the pork, garnish and serve with the vegetables and sauce.

Serves 6-8.

CARAWAY POT ROAST

1 tablespoon olive oil
1.25 kg (2¾ lb) hand of pork, boned
2 large onions, chopped
450 g (1 lb) parsnips, cut into chunks
25 g (1 oz) caraway seeds
½ teaspoon freshly grated nutmeg
salt and freshly ground black pepper
250 ml (9 fl oz/1 cup) chicken stock
250 ml (9 fl oz/1 cup) red wine
thyme sprigs, to garnish

Preheat oven to 180C (350F/Gas 4). Heat the oil in a large flameproof casserole. Add the pork and cook until browned all over.

Remove the meat from the casserole. Add the onions and parsnips and cook, stirring occasionally, for 7 minutes, until golden. Lay the pork on top of the vegetables. Mix together the caraway seeds and nutmeg and sprinkle on top of the pork. Season with salt and pepper. Pour the stock and wine around the pork. Cover tightly and cook in the oven for 2 hours, or until the pork is cooked through and tender. Remove the pork from the casserole and keep warm.

Remove the vegetables from the casserole with a slotted spoon. Bring the sauce to the boil and boil until reduced and thickened. Season with salt and pepper. Slice the meat, garnish with thyme sprigs and serve with the vegetables and sauce.

Serves 6-8.

Note: Hand of pork is quite a fatty cut of meat. Skim any fat from the surface of the sauce before serving, if you prefer.

──PROVENÇAL PORK CHOPS──

2 teaspoons capers, chopped
25 g (1 oz) pitted black olives, chopped
8 sun-dried tomatoes, chopped
50 g (2 oz) can anchovies, drained and chopped
juice of 2 lemons
2 cloves garlic, crushed
70 ml (2½ fl oz/⅓ cup) olive oil
4 tablespoons chopped fresh parsley
salt and freshly ground black pepper
4 x 175 g (6 oz) pork loin chops
basil sprigs, to garnish

Mix together the capers, olives, tomatoes, anchovies and lemon juice. Add the garlic, all but 1 tablespoon of the olive oil, the parsley and salt and pepper.

Heat the remaining oil in a flameproof dish. Add the chops and cook for 10 minutes on each side, until cooked through.

Pour the tomato mixture over the chops and bring to the boil. Simmer for 5 minutes. Garnish with basil sprigs and serve.

Serves 4.

—— PORK WITH APPLE BALLS ——

2 tablespoons olive oil
4 x 175 g (6 oz) boneless pork loin chops
450 g (1 lb) onions, sliced
2 cloves garlic, crushed
12 plum tomatoes, peeled and chopped
150 ml (5 fl oz/²⁄₃ cup) beef stock
55 ml (2 fl oz/¼ cup) red wine vinegar
700 g (1½ lb) crisp eating apples
2 tablespoons lemon juice
salt and freshly ground black pepper

Preheat oven to 180C (350F/Gas 4). Heat the olive oil in an ovenproof casserole. Add the chops and cook for 3 minutes on each side, until browned.

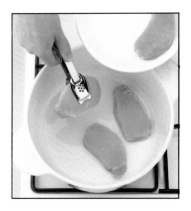

Remove the chops and keep warm. Add the onions to the casserole and cook, stirring occasionally, for 5 minutes, until soft. Add the garlic and tomatoes. Return the chops to the casserole and pour in the stock and red wine vinegar. Bring to the boil. Meanwhile, peel the apples and use a melon baller to cut out ball-shaped pieces. Put the balls into a bowl of water with the lemon juice, to prevent the apple discolouring. Chop the remaining apple and add to the casserole. Cover and cook in the oven for 1 hour.

Remove the chops from the casserole and keep warm. Pour the sauce into a blender or food processor and process for 1 minute. Season with salt and pepper. Return to the pan with the chops and apple balls. Cook gently for 15 minutes, until the apple balls are just tender. Serve.

Serves 4.

—————BARBECUE SPARE RIBS—————

1 kg (2¼ lb) spare ribs
1 large onion, finely chopped
3 cloves garlic, crushed
2 bay leaves
1 teaspoon ground cumin
1 teaspoon mild chilli powder
3 tablespoons cider vinegar
2 tablespoons tomato ketchup
1 tablespoon soy sauce
2 tablespoons clear honey
400 g (14 oz) can chopped tomatoes
salt and freshly ground black pepper

Preheat oven to 200C (400F/Gas 6). Put the spare ribs in a flameproof casserole and cook in the oven for 30 minutes.

Remove the ribs with a slotted spoon and set aside. In a bowl, mix together the onion, garlic, bay leaves, cumin, chilli powder, cider vinegar, tomato ketchup, soy sauce, honey and tomatoes. Season with salt and pepper.

Stir the tomato mixture into the casserole. Bring to the boil and simmer for 5 minutes. Add the ribs, turn to coat with the sauce and cover. Return the casserole to the oven and cook for 30 minutes. Serve.

Serves 4.

Variation: Use 4 spare rib pork chops instead of the spare ribs, if you prefer.

FRAGRANT GAMMON

1.35 kg (3 lb) piece of gammon
225 g (8 oz) parsnips, halved lengthways
450 g (1 lb) carrots, cut into chunks
450 g (1 lb) swede, cut into chunks
2 sticks celery, cut into chunks
1 tablespoon brown sugar
1 tablespoon red wine vinegar
1 tablespoon black peppercorns
6 cloves
oregano sprigs, to garnish

Put the gammon in a flameproof casserole. Cover with cold water and leave to soak for 1 hour. Drain and cover with fresh water.

Add the remaining ingredients to the casserole. Bring to the boil, cover and simmer gently for 1½ hours, until the gammon is cooked through.

Lift out the gammon, slice and arrange on warmed serving plates. Remove the vegetables with a slotted spoon, arrange around the gammon, garnish with oregano sprigs and serve.

Serves 6-8.

──FRUITY GAMMON STEAKS──

1 cm (½ in) piece fresh root ginger, peeled and
  grated
2 tablespoons tomato ketchup
1 tablespoon soft brown sugar
1 tablespoon light soy sauce
1 tablespoon malt vinegar
1 tablespoon lemon juice
2 tablespoons olive oil
4 x 175 g (6 oz) gammon steaks
1 green pepper (capsicum), chopped
1 red pepper (capsicum), chopped
1 onion, chopped
225 g (8 oz) can pineapple pieces, drained, with 2
  tablespoons juice reserved
1 tablespoon cornflour
watercress, to garnish

In a bowl, mix together the ginger, tomato
ketchup, brown sugar, soy sauce, vinegar and
lemon juice. Set aside. Heat the oil in a
flameproof dish. Add the gammon steaks
and cook for 5 minutes on each side.

Remove the steaks from the dish and keep
warm. Add the peppers (capsicum) and
onion to the dish and cook, stirring
occasionally, for 5 minutes, until soft. Stir in
the tomato ketchup mixture and the
pineapple pieces. Blend the reserved
pineapple juice with the cornflour. Add to
the dish and bring to the boil, stirring.
Return the steaks to the dish and simmer for
5 minutes. Garnish and serve.

Serves 4.

—COURGETTE & BACON SLICE—

450 g (1 lb) courgettes (zucchini), finely grated
1 large onion, finely chopped
6 rashers streaky bacon, chopped
150 g (5 oz/1 ¼ cups) grated mature Cheddar cheese
150 g (5 oz/1 ¼ cups) self-raising flour
150 ml (5 fl oz/⅔ cup) sunflower oil, plus extra for
    greasing
5 eggs, beaten
salt and freshly ground black pepper

Preheat oven to 200C (400F/Gas 6). In a large
bowl, mix together the courgettes (zucchini),
onion, bacon, cheese, flour, oil and eggs.
Season with salt and pepper.

Lightly grease a shallow flameproof dish.
Add the courgette (zucchini) mixture and
level the surface. Bake for 50-60 minutes,
until golden brown and firm. Cut into
wedges and serve hot or cold.

Serves 4-6.

──STUFFED CABBAGE LEAVES──

18 large cabbage leaves
2 onions, finely chopped
4 tablespoons finely chopped fresh parsley
2 cloves garlic, crushed
225 g (8 oz) young spinach, shredded
225 g (8 oz) minced pork
450 g (1 lb) pork sausagemeat
25 g (1 oz/¼ cup) plain flour
2 eggs, beaten
salt and freshly ground black pepper
12 rashers streaky bacon
500 ml (18 fl oz/2¼ cups) chicken stock

Blanch the cabbage leaves in boiling water for 2 minutes. Remove and drain.

Preheat oven to 180C (350F/Gas 4). In a large bowl, mix together the onions, parsley, garlic, spinach, pork and sausagemeat. Add the flour and eggs and mix well. Season with salt and pepper. Divide into six portions. Trim the tough central core from each cabbage leaf. Arrange the leaves in six piles of three leaves each.

Divide the portions of filling among the cabbage leaves. Fold each one into a parcel and wrap each one with two rashers of bacon. Put into an flameproof casserole and pour over the stock. Bring to the boil, cover and cook in the oven for 1½ hours. Remove with a slotted spoon, pour over a little of the cooking liquid and serve.

Serves 6.

——————TOAD IN THE HOLE——————

115 g (4oz/1 cup) plain flour
pinch of salt
1 teaspoon mixed dried herbs
1 egg, beaten
300 ml (10 fl oz/1¼ cups) milk
1 tablespoon sunflower oil
1 small onion, chopped
450 g (1 lb) herby sausages

Preheat oven to 200C (400F/Gas 6). In a large
bowl, mix together the flour, salt and herbs.
Make a well in the centre and add the egg and
half of the milk. Beat to a smooth batter. Stir
in the remaining milk and mix until smooth.

Heat the oil in a shallow flameproof dish.
Add the onion and cook, stirring
occasionally, for 3 minutes. Add the sausages
and cook until browned all over.

Pour the batter into the dish and cook in the
oven for 30 minutes, until the batter is risen
and golden. Serve immediately.

Serves 4.

Variation: There are many types of flavoured
sausages available. Try using different types
to vary this recipe.

—————LAMB EN PAPILLOTTE—————

4 x 175 g (6 oz) lamb leg steaks
1 tablespoon Dijon mustard
4 spring onions, sliced
1 teaspoon chopped fresh rosemary
salt and freshly ground black pepper
450 g (1 lb) sweet potatoes, cut into chunks
450 g (1 lb) courgettes (zucchini), thickly sliced
1 tablespoon olive oil
rosemary sprigs, to garnish

Preheat oven to 200C (400F/Gas 6). Cut four large squares of foil and place a lamb steak on each one. Spread the lamb with the mustard and sprinkle with the spring onions and rosemary. Season with salt and pepper.

Bring the foil up over the steaks to make a parcel and twist the edges together to seal. Put the parcels in an ovenproof dish. Arrange the sweet potatoes and courgettes (zucchini) around the parcels.

Drizzle with oil and season with salt and pepper. Cook in the oven for 1 hour, basting and turning the vegetables at least twice. Remove the lamb from the parcels, garnish with rosemary and serve with the vegetables.

Serves 4.

──ORANGE & GINGER LAMB──

2 tablespoons dark soy sauce
2 tablespoons dry sherry
1 tablespoon orange juice
2 cloves garlic, finely chopped
1 cm (½ in) piece fresh root ginger, peeled and
  grated
450 g (1 lb) lamb fillet, cut into strips
2 tablespoons vegetable oil
115 g (4 oz) broccoli flowerets
225 g (8 oz) carrots, cut into matchsticks
1 red pepper (capsicum), thinly sliced
1 teaspoon soft brown sugar
coriander sprigs, to garnish

In a bowl, mix together the soy sauce, sherry, orange juice, garlic and ginger. Add the lamb.

Turn to coat with the marinade and leave to marinate for 2-3 hours. Drain the lamb, reserving the marinade. Heat the oil in a flameproof dish or casserole. Add the lamb and cook, stirring, for 8-10 minutes, until browned all over and cooked through. Add the broccoli, carrots and pepper (capsicum) and cook, stirring, for 5 minutes.

Pour in the reserved marinade and sugar and bring to the boil. Cover and simmer gently for 5 minutes. Garnish with coriander sprigs and serve immediately.

Serves 4.

—CHUMP CHOP BOULANGÈRE—

1 tablespoon olive oil
4 x 175 g (6 oz) lamb chump chops
2 large onions, sliced
225 g (8 oz) Savoy cabbage, shredded
450 g (1 lb) old potatoes, thinly sliced
salt and freshly ground black pepper
fresh bouquet garni
500 ml (18 fl oz/2¼ cups) lamb or chicken stock
25 g (1 oz/ 2 tablespoons) butter, melted
chopped fresh parsley, to garnish

Heat the oil in a flameproof casserole. Add the chops and cook for 2-3 minutes on each side until browned. Remove and set aside.

Preheat oven to 200C (400F/Gas 6). Add the onions and cabbage to the casserole and cook gently for 10 minutes, until soft. Remove half the mixture and set aside. Place the chops on top of the remaining onion and cabbage mixture. Mix two-thirds of the potatoes with the reserved onion and cabbage mixture. Season with salt and pepper. Arrange on top of the chops, placing the bouquet garni in the middle. Pour over the stock.

Arrange the remaining potatoes on top and brush with melted butter. Cook in the oven for 15 minutes. Remove from the oven and press the potatoes down. Brush again with melted butter and season with salt and pepper. Lower the oven temperature to 180C (350F/Gas 4) and cook for 1 hour. Garnish with chopped parsley and serve.

Serves 4.

MEDITERRANEAN LAMB

1 aubergine (eggplant), sliced
2 teaspoons salt
2 tablespoons olive oil, plus extra for brushing
450 g (1 lb) lamb fillet, cubed
2 leeks, sliced
1 green pepper (capsicum), chopped
400 g (14 oz) can chopped tomatoes
1 clove garlic, crushed
2 courgettes (zucchini), sliced
1 tablespoon tomato purée (paste)
1 tablespoon chopped fresh rosemary

Place the aubergine (eggplant) in a colander, sprinkle with the salt and leave to stand for 30 minutes.

Preheat oven to 190C (375F/Gas 5). Heat the oil in a flameproof dish. Add the lamb and cook, stirring, for 3-4 minutes, until browned all over. Add the leeks and cook, stirring, for 4-5 minutes, until soft. Stir in the pepper (capsicum), tomatoes, garlic, courgettes (zucchini), tomato purée (paste) and rosemary. Simmer for 5-10 minutes.

Rinse the aubergine (eggplant) in cold water and pat dry with kitchen paper. Arrange the aubergine (eggplant) slices on top of the lamb mixture and brush with olive oil. Bake for 30-40 minutes, until the aubergine (eggplant) slices are golden brown and tender. Serve.

Serves 4.

–RACK OF LAMB WITH ONIONS–

grated rind of 1 lemon
1 tablespoon chopped fresh parsley
2 teaspoons garlic purée
1 tablespoon chopped fresh rosemary
salt and freshly ground black pepper
8-bone rack of lamb
8 small onions, peeled
1 tablespoon olive oil
250 ml (9 fl oz/1 cup) lamb or vegetable stock
3 tablespoons red wine vinegar
2 tablespoons caster sugar
rosemary sprigs, to garnish

Preheat oven to 200C (400F/Gas 6). In a small bowl, mix together the lemon rind, parsley, garlic purée, rosemary and salt and pepper.

Put the lamb, fat side up, in a flameproof dish. Spread the lemon and herb mixture over the lamb. Place the onions in the dish and brush with the oil. Roast for 20 minutes. Turn off the heat and leave the lamb and onions in the oven for 20 minutes. Remove from the dish and keep warm.

Add the stock, vinegar and caster sugar to the dish. Season with plenty of black pepper. Bring to the boil and boil, stirring, until the liquid has reduced by half and thickened. Return the onions to the dish, turn in the sauce and simmer for 5 minutes. Cut the lamb into individual chops, garnish and serve with the onions and sauce.

Serves 4.

Note: If you prefer, roast the lamb for an extra 5-10 minutes, according to taste.

SAGE LAMB COBBLER

900 g (2 lb) neck of lamb, boned and cubed
25 g (1 oz/¼ cup) plain flour
1 tablespoon olive oil
1 large onion, chopped
55 g (2 oz/¼ cup) dried peas, soaked overnight
225 g (8 oz) each carrots and swede, diced
500 ml (18 fl oz/2¼ cups) lamb or chicken stock
salt and freshly ground black pepper
large pinch of paprika
TOPPING:
225 g (8 oz/2 cups) plain flour
1½ teaspoons baking powder
55 g (2 oz/¼ cup) butter
1 teaspoon dried sage
1 egg
2 tablespoons milk, plus extra for brushing

Preheat oven to 160C (325F/Gas 3). Coat the lamb in the flour. Heat the oil in a flameproof casserole. Add the lamb and cook until browned all over. Remove and set aside. Add the onion and cook, stirring occasionally, for 7 minutes, until lightly browned. Return the lamb and add the peas, carrots and swede. Pour in the stock and season with salt, pepper and paprika. Bring to the boil, cover and cook in the oven for 2 hours. Sift the flour, baking powder and salt into a bowl. Rub in the butter until the mixture resembles fine breadcrumbs.

Stir in the sage. Add the egg and milk and bind to a soft dough. Knead on a lightly floured surface and roll out to 1 cm (½ in) thick. Using a pastry cutter, cut out 4 cm (1½ in) rounds. Arrange the scones on top of the casserole and brush with milk. Increase the oven temperature to 200C (400F/Gas 6). Return the casserole to the oven and cook, uncovered, for 15-20 minutes, until the scones are risen and golden. Serve.

Serves 6-8.

——VEAL WITH MUSHROOMS——

2 tablespoons olive oil
6 rashers streaky bacon, cut into thin strips
4 x 225 g (8 oz) slices veal shank
350 g (12 oz) carrots, cut into thick strips
4 plum tomatoes, peeled, quartered and seeded
550 ml (20 fl oz/2½ cups) beef stock
115 ml (4 fl oz/½ cup) red wine
450 g (1 lb) mixed mushrooms
55 g (2 oz/¼ cup) butter, diced
55 g (2 oz) chopped fresh parsley

Heat the oil in a flameproof casserole. Add the bacon and cook for 3-4 minutes. Remove and drain on kitchen paper. Add the veal and cook until browned on both sides.

Remove the veal and drain on kitchen paper. Add the carrots and tomatoes to the casserole and cook for 2-3 minutes. Return the veal to the casserole. Pour over the stock and the red wine. Bring to the boil, cover and simmer for 40 minutes. Add the mushrooms and bacon and cook for 10 minutes, until the veal is cooked through and tender.

Lift out the veal and remove the carrots, mushrooms and bacon with a slotted spoon. Keep warm. Strain the sauce and return to the casserole. Bring to the boil and boil until reduced by one-third. Whisk in the butter, a little at a time. Stir in the parsley. Return the bacon and vegetables to the sauce and cook gently for 2 minutes, to warm through. Arrange the veal on warmed serving plates, pour the sauce over and serve.

Serves 4.

BAKED EGGS IN NESTS

700 g (1½ lb) waxy potatoes, halved
225 g (8 oz) broccoli flowerets
2 courgettes (zucchini)
2 leeks, thinly sliced
1 tablespoon Worcestershire sauce
salt and freshly ground black pepper
vegetable oil for greasing
4 eggs

Cook the potatoes in boiling salted water for 5-10 minutes. Add the broccoli and cook for 5 minutes. Drain.

Coarsely grate the potatoes. Using a vegetable peeler, cut the courgettes (zucchini) lengthwise into ribbons. Mix together the potatoes, broccoli, leeks, courgettes (zucchini) and Worcestershire sauce. Season with salt and pepper. Lightly oil a flameproof casserole and add the vegetable mixture.

Make four wells in the vegetable mixture and break an egg into each one. Cover and cook very gently for 10 minutes, until the eggs have set. Serve immediately.

Serves 2-4.

—FENNEL & BEAN CASSEROLE—

300 g (10 oz/1¼ cups) dried haricot beans, soaked
  overnight
1 tablespoon olive oil
2 onions, chopped
2 cloves garlic, crushed
1 head of celery, sliced
2 fennel bulbs, thinly sliced
2 tablespoons tomato purée (paste)
2 tablespoons chopped fresh oregano
1 tablespoon chopped fresh thyme
2 bay leaves
2 teaspoons each salt and sugar
2 x 400 g (14 oz) cans chopped tomatoes
freshly ground black pepper
6 slices day-old bread, made into crumbs
thyme sprigs, to garnish

Put the haricot beans in a flameproof
casserole. Cover with cold water. Bring to the
boil and boil rapidly for 10 minutes. Cover
and simmer for 1 hour. Drain and set aside.
Heat the oil in the casserole. Add the onions
and garlic and cook, stirring occasionally, for
5 minutes, until soft. Add the beans, celery,
fennel, tomato purée (paste), half of the
oregano, the thyme, bay leaves, salt, sugar
and tomatoes. Season with black pepper.
Cover and simmer for 30 minutes.

Preheat oven to 220C (425F/Gas 7). Mix
together the breadcrumbs and remaining
oregano and scatter over the top of the bean
mixture. Cook for 15-20 minutes, until the
breadcrumbs are golden brown. Garnish
with thyme sprigs and serve.

Serves 4-6.

LEEK & CHEESE PIE

450 g (1 lb) leeks, chopped
1 teaspoon salt
55 g (2 oz/¼ cup) butter
2 large onions, sliced
2 bunches spring onions, sliced
115 g (4 oz/1 cup) crumbled feta cheese
2 eggs, beaten
freshly ground black pepper
2 tablespoons olive oil
8 sheets filo pastry
55 g (2 oz/¼ cup) melted butter

Put the leeks into a colander, sprinkle with
salt and leave for 30 minutes. Squeeze dry.

Heat the butter in a flameproof dish. Add the
onions and spring onions and cook, stirring
occasionally, for 3-5 minutes, until soft but
not coloured. Remove from the heat and
leave to cool for 10 minutes. Preheat oven to
200C (400F/Gas 6). Add the leeks, feta cheese
and eggs to the onion mixture, season with
black pepper and mix well.

Crumple the sheets of filo pastry and arrange
on top of the leek mixture. Brush with
melted butter and bake for 30-35 minutes,
until the pastry is golden brown. Serve.

Serves 4-6.

VEGETABLE BIRYANI

2 tablespoons sunflower oil
450 g (1 lb) onions, sliced
300 g (10 oz) carrots, diced
115 g (4 oz) potatoes, diced
2.5 cm (1 in) piece fresh root ginger, peeled and grated
2 cloves garlic, crushed
1 tablespoon hot curry paste
1 teaspoon turmeric
½ teaspoon ground cinnamon
225 g (8 oz/1 cup) long grain rice
1 litre (35 fl oz/4¼ cups) hot vegetable stock
115 g (4 oz) cauliflower flowerets
salt and freshly ground black pepper
115 g (4 oz) frozen peas
55 g (2 oz/½ cup) toasted cashew nuts
2 tablespoons chopped fresh coriander

Heat half the oil in a large flameproof casserole. Add half the onions and cook, stirring occasionally, for 10-15 minutes, until crisp and golden. Remove with a slotted spoon, drain on kitchen paper and set aside. Heat the remaining oil in the casserole and add the carrots, potatoes and remaining onions. Stir in the ginger, garlic, curry paste, turmeric and cinnamon and cook, stirring, for 5 minutes.

Add the rice and stir for 1 minute. Pour in the stock and bring to the boil. Stir in the cauliflower and salt and pepper. Cover and simmer gently for 15 minutes. Stir in the peas, cashews and coriander. Cover and cook for 5 minutes until the rice is tender and the liquid has been absorbed. Scatter the reserved onions over the top and serve.

Serves 4.

———— COURGETTE GOUGÈRE ————

2 tablespoons olive oil
5 courgettes (zucchini), thinly sliced
300 g (10 oz) button mushrooms
2 leeks, thinly sliced
2 teaspoons wholegrain mustard
300 ml (10 fl oz/1¼ cups) crème fraîche
salt and freshly ground black pepper
CHOUX PASTRY:
55 g (2 oz/¼ cup) butter
225 g (8 oz/2 cups) plain flour
2 eggs, beaten

To make the choux pastry, gently melt the butter in 150 ml (5 fl oz/⅔ cup) water, then bring quickly to the boil. Remove from the heat and immediately stir in the flour.

Beat well until the mixture is smooth and comes away from the sides of the pan. Return to the heat and cook gently, stirring, for 2-3 minutes. Remove from the heat and gradually add the eggs, beating well. Set aside. Preheat oven to 220C (425F/Gas 7). Heat the oil in a flameproof casserole. Add the courgettes (zucchini), button mushrooms and leeks and cook, stirring occasionally, for 6-8 minutes, until tender.

Stir in the mustard and crème fraîche and season with salt and pepper. Put the choux pastry in a piping bag fitted with a plain 1 cm (½ in) nozzle. Pipe small balls of pastry around the edge of the courgette (zucchini) mixture. Bake for 20-30 minutes, until the pastry is risen and golden. Serve.

Serves 4-6.

— SAVOURY BREAD PUDDING —

6 thick slices wholemeal bread
2 courgettes (zucchini), sliced
1 beefsteak tomato, chopped
175 g (6 oz) mushrooms, chopped
400 ml (14 fl oz/1¾ cups) milk
5 eggs, beaten
1 tablespoon chopped fresh chives
salt and freshly ground black pepper
150 g (5 oz/1¼ cups) grated Cheddar cheese
flat-leaf parsley sprigs, to garnish

Preheat oven to 200C (400F/Gas 6). Cut the bread into fingers. Arrange half the fingers in a shallow ovenproof dish.

Spread the courgettes (zucchini), tomatoes and mushrooms over the bread and top with the remaining bread. In a large bowl, mix together the milk and eggs. Add the chives and season with salt and pepper.

Pour the milk mixture over the bread. Sprinkle the cheese over the top and bake for 50 minutes, until the egg mixture has set and the topping is golden brown. Garnish with flat-leaf parsley and serve.

Serves 4.

MOROCCAN CASSEROLE

2 tablespoons olive oil
1 large onion, chopped
1 large aubergine (eggplant), cut into chunks
2 cloves garlic, crushed
1 teaspoon ground cumin
1 teaspoon turmeric
1 teaspoon ground ginger
1 teaspoon paprika
1 teaspoon ground allspice
3 x 400 g (14 oz) cans chopped tomatoes
450 g (1 lb) can chick peas, drained
75 g (3 oz) raisins
1 tablespoon chopped fresh coriander
3 tablespoons chopped fresh parsley
salt and freshly ground black pepper

Heat the oil in a flameproof casserole. Add the onion and cook, stirring occasionally, for 5 minutes, until soft. Add the aubergine (eggplant), cover and cook for 5 minutes. Add the garlic, ground cumin, turmeric, ground ginger, paprika and allspice and cook, stirring, for 1 minute.

Stir in the tomatoes, chick peas, raisins and chopped coriander and parsley. Season with salt and pepper. Bring to the boil and simmer for 45 minutes. Serve.

Serves 4-6.

—MUSHROOM & NUT PILAU—

45 g (1½ oz/3 tablespoons) butter
55 g (2 oz) pine nuts
55 g (2 oz) sunflower seeds
1 onion, chopped
2 leeks, chopped
1 red pepper (capsicum), chopped
1 carrot, diced
225 g (8 oz/1 cup) risotto rice
1 litre (35 fl oz/4½ cups) vegetable stock
115 g (4 oz) button mushrooms, sliced
salt and freshly ground black pepper

Heat 15 g (½ oz) of the butter in a flameproof casserole. Add the pine nuts and sunflower seeds and cook until golden.

Remove from the casserole with a slotted spoon and set aside. Heat the remaining butter in the casserole. Add the onion, leeks, pepper (capsicum) and carrot and cook, stirring occasionally, for 3 minutes. Add the rice and cook, stirring, for 2 minutes. Add the stock, cover and bring to the boil. Simmer for 30 minutes, until most of the liquid is absorbed and the rice is just tender.

Add the mushrooms, pine nuts and sunflower seeds and cook gently, stirring frequently, for 10 minutes. Season with salt and pepper and serve.

Serves 4.

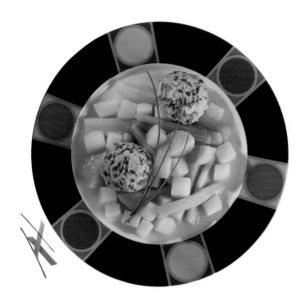

– LEEK STEW WITH DUMPLINGS –

700 g (1½ lb) leeks, halved lengthways
350 g (12 oz) potatoes, diced
225 g (8 oz) Jerusalem artichokes, peeled and
   quartered
1 litre (35 fl oz/4½ cups) vegetable stock
salt
fresh chives, to garnish
DUMPLINGS:
115 g (4 oz/1 cup) self-raising flour
55 g (2 oz) vegetable suet
25 g (1 oz) chopped fresh chives

Cut the leeks into 7.5 cm (3 in) lengths. Put the leeks, potatoes and artichokes in a large flameproof casserole.

Add the stock and season with salt. Bring to the boil, cover and simmer for 45-60 minutes. Meanwhile, to make the dumplings, put the flour, suet, and chives in a large bowl, season with salt and mix well. Stir in 55 ml (2 fl oz/ ¼ cup) water and bind to a dough. Knead lightly and leave to rest for 5 minutes.

Shape the dough into eight small dumplings. Place the dumplings around the outside of the vegetable mixture. Cover and simmer for 30 minutes. Garnish with chives and serve.

Serves 4.

—STIR-FRIED SPINACH & TOFU—

1 tablespoon olive oil
2 sticks celery, sliced
10 spring onions, sliced
2.5 cm (1 in) piece fresh root ginger, peeled and
    thinly sliced
225 g (8 oz) smoked tofu
175 g (6 oz) mange tout (snow peas)
450 g (1 lb) spinach, roughly torn
1 tablespoon black bean sauce
freshly ground black pepper
2 tablespoons toasted sesame seeds

Heat the oil in a flameproof casserole. Add
the celery, spring onions and ginger and stir-
fry for 3-4 minutes, until soft.

Add the tofu and mange tout (snow peas) and
stir-fry for 2-3 minutes. Gradually add the
spinach and stir-fry for 8-10 minutes, until
wilted and tender.

Stir in the black bean sauce and mix well.
Season with black pepper. Stir in the sesame
seeds and serve.

Serves 4.

VEGETABLE COBBLER

1 tablespoon olive oil
1 clove garlic, crushed
2 leeks, thinly sliced
2 teaspoons mustard seeds
225 g (8 oz) mushrooms, sliced
225 g (8 oz) broccoli flowerets
175 g (6 oz) fresh or frozen peas
300 ml (10 fl oz/1¼ cups) single (light) cream
large pinch of freshly grated nutmeg
1 teaspoon prepared English mustard
1 tablespoon chopped fresh parsley
200 g (7 oz) puff pastry, thawed if frozen
milk for brushing

Heat the oil in a flameproof casserole. Add the garlic and leeks and cook until soft.

Add the mustard seeds and cook until they start to pop. Add the mushrooms, broccoli and peas. Cover and cook for 8-10 minutes, until tender. Remove from the heat. Stir in the cream, nutmeg, mustard and parsley. Preheat oven to 220C (425F/Gas 7).

Roll out the pastry on a lightly floured surface. Using a pastry cutter, cut out twelve 5 cm (2 in) rounds. Arrange on top of the vegetable mixture. Brush with a little milk and bake for 30-35 minutes, until risen and golden. Serve.

Serves 4-6.

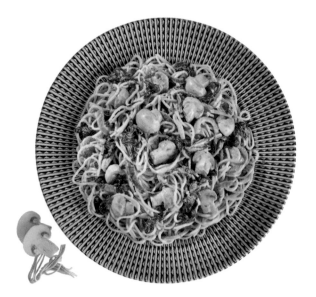

NOODLES WITH SPINACH

2 tablespoons olive oil
1 red onion, thinly sliced
300 g (10 oz) button mushrooms, halved
350 g (12 oz) spinach, roughly torn
225 g (8 oz) thread egg noodles
225 g (8 oz/1 cup) soft cheese with garlic and herbs
salt and freshly ground black pepper

Heat the oil in a flameproof casserole. Add the onion and cook, stirring occasionally, for 5 minutes, until soft. Add the mushrooms and spinach and cook, stirring occasionally, for 10-15 minutes, until the spinach is wilted and the mushrooms tender.

Meanwhile, put the noodles in a large bowl and cover with boiling water. Leave for 4-5 minutes, until tender. Drain. Add the garlic and herb cheese to the spinach mixture and heat gently, stirring, until melted.

Add the noodles to the vegetable and cheese, season with salt and pepper and mix well. Serve.

Serves 4.

SPANISH OMELETTE

2 tablespoons olive oil
1 onion, thinly sliced
350 g (12 oz) potatoes, diced
1 red pepper (capsicum), thinly sliced
1 green pepper (capsicum), thinly sliced
6 eggs, beaten
1 tablespoon chopped fresh parsley
salt and freshly ground black pepper

Heat the oil in a shallow flameproof dish. Add the onion and potatoes and cook, stirring occasionally, for 6-8 minutes, until the potatoes are tender. Stir in the peppers (capsicum) and cook for 2-3 minutes.

Beat together the eggs, parsley and salt and pepper and pour into the dish. Cook gently for 3-4 minutes, until the eggs have set on the bottom. Preheat the grill.

Put the omelette under the grill and cook for 5-6 minutes, until the eggs have set. Cut into wedges and serve hot or at room temperature.

Serves 4.

——MIXED VEGETABLE RÖSTI——

1 tablespoon olive oil
1 onion, sliced
225 g (8 oz) green beans, trimmed
225 g (8 oz) cauliflower flowerets
4 tomatoes, peeled and quartered
1 tablespoon chopped fresh parsley
salt and freshly ground black pepper
700 g (1½ lb) potatoes, grated
115 g (4 oz/1 cup) grated mozzarella cheese

Heat the oil in a flameproof dish. Add the sliced onion and cook, stirring occasionally, for 5 minutes, until soft. Preheat oven to 200C (400F/Gas 6).

Add the beans, cauliflower and tomatoes and cook, stirring occasionally, for 10 minutes, until tender. Stir in the parsley and season with salt and pepper.

Spread the potatoes over the vegetables and top with cheese. Bake for 30 minutes, until the potatoes are tender and the cheese is melted and golden. Serve.

Serves 4.

Note: Waxy potatoes, such as Maris Piper, should be used for this recipe.

──SPICED FRUITY COUSCOUS──

2 tablespoons olive oil
25 g (1 oz/2 tablespoons) butter
6 spring onions, finely chopped
450 ml (16 fl oz/2 cups) vegetable stock
2 tablespoons Malaysian curry blend
1 teaspoon sugar
225 g (8 oz/generous cup) couscous
2 tablespoons chopped fresh chives
55 g (2 oz) green eating apples, cored and finely
    diced
55 g (2 oz) pine nuts

Heat the oil and butter in a flameproof casserole. Add the spring onions and cook gently until soft. Add the stock, curry blend and sugar.

Bring to the boil. Add the couscous and stir well. Put the lid on the casserole, turn off the heat and leave to stand for 30 minutes, until the stock has been absorbed and the couscous is tender.

Add the chives, apples and pine nuts and stir well. Serve immediately.

Serves 2-4.

Note: If Malaysian curry blend is not available, use a mild curry powder instead.

—NUT BAKE WITH TOMATOES—

25 g (1 oz/ 2 tablespoons) butter
1 onion, finely chopped
150 g (5 oz) carrot, finely chopped
2 sticks celery, finely chopped
300 g (10 oz/2½ cups) finely chopped mixed nuts
115 g (4 oz/2 cups) fresh wholemeal breadcrumbs
2 teaspoons yeast extract
300 ml (10 fl oz/1¼ cups) hot vegetable stock
2 teaspoons dried thyme
salt and freshly ground black pepper
2 beefsteak tomatoes, sliced
115 g (4 oz/1 cup) grated mature Cheddar cheese

Preheat oven to 180C (350F/Gas 4). Heat the butter in a flameproof casserole.

Add the onion, carrot and celery and cook gently, stirring occasionally, for 10 minutes, until soft. In a large bowl, mix together the nuts and breadcrumbs. Stir in the cooked vegetables. Dissolve the yeast extract in the hot stock and stir into the bowl. Add the thyme and season with salt and pepper. Mix well. Arrange half the tomato slices in the base of the casserole. Sprinkle with half of the grated cheese.

Spread half of the nut mixture on top. Add the remaining tomato slices and cover with the remaining nut mixture. Sprinkle with the remaining grated cheese and bake for 50-60 minutes, until the cheese is melted and golden. Serve.

Serves 4.

–SUN-DRIED TOMATO RISOTTO–

55 g (2 oz/¼ cup) butter
1 tablespoon olive oil
2 red onions, chopped
12 sun-dried tomatoes, chopped
3 teaspoons pesto sauce
225 g (8 oz/1 cup) risotto rice
1 litre (35 fl oz/4½ cups) vegetable stock
225 g (8 oz) mushrooms, sliced
salt and freshly ground black pepper
55 g (2 oz) Parmesan cheese
chopped fresh flat-leaf parsley, to garnish

Heat the butter and oil in a flameproof casserole. Add the onions and cook, stirring occasionally, for 5 minutes, until soft.

Add the sun-dried tomatoes and pesto sauce and cook for 3-4 minutes. Add the rice and cook, stirring, for 1 minute. Stir in about one-third of the stock and simmer gently, stirring occasionally, until most of the liquid has been absorbed.

Stir in the mushrooms and season with salt and pepper. Add half of the remaining stock and simmer, stirring occasionally. When most of the liquid has been absorbed, stir in the remaining stock and simmer gently until all the liquid has been absorbed and the rice is tender and creamy. Using a vegetable peeler, shave curls of Parmesan cheese over the risotto, sprinkle with parsley and serve.

Serves 2-4.

LENTIL & BEAN CHILLI

1 tablespoon olive oil
1 onion, chopped
1 clove garlic, chopped
175 g (6 oz/¾ cup) green lentils
300 ml (10 fl oz/1¼ cups) vegetable stock
1 teaspoon mild chilli powder
400 g (14 oz) can chopped tomatoes
400 g (14 oz) can red kidney beans in chilli sauce
1 green pepper (capsicum), chopped
salt and freshly ground black pepper
chopped fresh flat-leaf parsley, to garnish

Heat the oil in a flameproof casserole and cook the onion and garlic until soft. Add the lentils, stock, chilli powder and tomatoes.

Cover and simmer gently for 30-40 minutes, until the lentils are almost cooked.

Stir in the kidney beans and their sauce and the green pepper (capsicum) and simmer for 10-15 minutes, until the lentils are cooked and the liquid has been absorbed. Season with salt and pepper. Garnish with chopped parsley and serve.

Serves 4.

——— SWEET PEPPER CHILLI ———

2 onions
5 large fresh red chillies, cored, seeded and chopped
1 red pepper (capsicum), chopped
1 large clove garlic, chopped
2 tablespoons dry white wine
salt
1 tablespoon olive oil
1 green pepper (capsicum), thinly sliced
1 tablespoon tomato purée (paste)
1 teaspoon ground cumin
200 g (7 oz) can red kidney beans, drained
basil sprigs, to garnish

Roughly chop one of the onions. Put in a food processor with the chillies, red pepper (capsicum), garlic, wine and salt.

Process for 2 minutes. Slice the remaining onion. Heat the oil in a flameproof casserole, add the sliced onion and cook, stirring occasionally, for 5 minutes, until soft. Add the puréed mixture, 2 tablespoons water and the green pepper (capsicum).

Bring to the boil, cover and simmer gently for 30 minutes. Add the tomato purée (paste), cumin and kidney beans. Simmer for 10-15 minutes. Garnish with basil and serve.

Serves 2-4.

——VEGETABLE FRICASSÉE——

400 ml (14 fl oz/1¾ cups) vegetable stock
350 g (12 oz) swede, cut into chunks
225 g (8 oz) each carrots and potatoes, cut into chunks
1 leek, sliced
225 g (8 oz) cauliflower flowerets
225 g (8 oz) green beans
55 g (2 oz/¼ cup) butter
55 g (2 oz/½ cup) wholemeal flour
150 ml (5 fl oz/⅔ cup) milk
6 tablespoons chopped fresh parsley
1 teaspoon lemon juice
salt and freshly ground black pepper

Put the stock in a flameproof casserole and bring to the boil. Add the swede, carrots and potatoes.

Return to the boil and cook for 5 minutes. Add the leek, cauliflower and beans and cook for 3-5 minutes. Drain the vegetables, reserving the stock. Heat the butter in the casserole. Add the flour and cook, stirring, for 1 minute. Gradually stir in the milk and 250 ml (9 fl oz/1 cup) of the reserved stock, stirring constantly until smooth.

Reduce the heat, stir in the parsley and lemon juice and season with salt and pepper. Add the vegetables and cook for 4-5 minutes, to warm through. Serve.

Serves 4.

——— MUSHROOM GRATIN ———

15 g (½ oz/1 tablespoon) butter
1 clove garlic, crushed
900 g (2 lb) potatoes, thinly sliced
175 g (6 oz) chestnut mushrooms, sliced
115 g (4 oz) button mushrooms, sliced
salt and freshly ground black pepper
2 eggs, beaten
150 ml (5 fl oz/⅔ cup) milk
150 ml (5 fl oz/⅔ cup) crème fraîche
175 g (6 oz/1½ cups) grated Gruyère cheese
chopped fresh parsley, to garnish

Preheat oven to 200C (400F/Gas 6). Rub an
ovenproof dish with the butter and garlic.
Add half the potatoes and the mushrooms.

Top with the remaining potatoes. Season
generously with salt and pepper. Mix
together the eggs, milk and crème fraîche and
pour over the vegetables. Bake for 1 hour.

Sprinkle the cheese over the top and bake for
25 minutes, until the cheese is melted and
golden. Garnish with parsley and serve.

Serves 4.

— BAKED PANETTONE PUDDING —

3 eggs, beaten
115 g (4 oz/½ cup) caster sugar
400 ml (14 fl oz/1¾ cups) full-fat milk
few drops of vanilla essence
butter for greasing
6 slices panettone with dried fruit
4 tablespoons marmalade
icing sugar for dusting

In a large bowl, beat the eggs and sugar until light and foamy. Add the milk and vanilla essence and mix well.

Lightly butter a shallow ovenproof dish. Spread the slices of panettone with the marmalade. Sandwich together, two pieces at a time and cut the pieces in half. Arrange in the dish. Ladle the custard mixture over the panettone and leave to soak for 15 minutes.

Preheat oven to 160C (325F/Gas 3). Place the dish in a larger ovenproof dish or roasting tin and pour in enough boiling water to come halfway up the sides of the dish. Bake for 50 minutes, until the custard is set and the top is golden with a slight crust. Sprinkle with icing sugar and serve hot or cold.

Serves 4-6.

Variation: For a more economical dessert, replace the panettone with slices of tea bread.

FLAMBÉED FRUIT

55 g (2 oz/¼ cup) butter
55 g (2 oz/¼ cup) caster sugar
2 oranges, peeled and segmented
350 g (12 oz) can pineapple pieces in natural juice
4 bananas, thickly sliced
1 tablespoon orange liqueur or brandy
mint sprigs, to garnish

Put the butter and sugar in a flameproof dish and cook over a gentle heat until they melt and turn a caramel colour.

Add the oranges, pineapple pieces and their juice and bananas. Bring to the boil and boil for 5 minutes, until the sauce thickens.

Put the liqueur or brandy in a ladle and warm gently. Set alight and pour over the fruit. Cook for 1 minute, until the flames die down. Garnish with mint and serve warm.

Serves 4.

——RHUBARB MERINGUE——

450 g (1 lb) rhubarb, sliced
4 bananas, sliced
55 g (2 oz/¼ cup) soft brown sugar
½ teaspoon ground cinnamon
grated rind and juice of 3 oranges
MERINGUE:
3 egg whites
175 g (6 oz/¾ cup) caster sugar

Preheat oven to 180C (350F/Gas 4). Put the rhubarb and bananas in an ovenproof dish. Sprinkle with brown sugar, cinnamon and orange rind. Pour over the orange juice, making sure the fruit is evenly coated.

Cover with a lid or piece of foil and bake for 15-20 minutes, until the fruit is tender. Meanwhile, to make the meringue, beat the egg whites until they form stiff peaks. Fold in the caster sugar.

Put the meringue in a piping bag and pipe over the fruit. Return to the oven and cook for 20 minutes, until the meringue is crisp and golden. Serve warm or cold.

Serves 4-6.

Note: If you prefer, you can simply spoon the meringue over the fruit.

——— BAKED APPLES IN BATTER ———

2 tablespoons golden syrup
4 sweet eating apples, cored
8 bay leaves
icing sugar for dusting
BATTER:
55 g (2 oz/½ cup) plain flour
2 eggs, beaten
few drops of vanilla essence
300 ml (10 fl oz/1¼ cups) milk
55 g (2 oz/¼ cup) caster sugar
15 g (½ oz/1 tablespoon) butter, melted, plus extra
  for greasing

Preheat oven to 190C (375F/Gas 5). Lightly butter an ovenproof dish and spread golden syrup over the base.

Place the apples on top of the golden syrup. Put a bay leaf in the cavity of each apple, reserving the four remaining leaves for decoration. Bake for 15 minutes. Meanwhile, make the batter. Sift the flour into a large bowl and make a well in the centre. Add the eggs, vanilla essence and a little milk. Beat into the flour, gradually adding more milk to form a smooth batter. Stir in the caster sugar and melted butter.

Pour the batter over the apples and bake for 45-50 minutes, until the batter is risen and golden. Remove the bay leaves from the apples. Decorate with the reserved bay leaves, dust with icing sugar and serve.

Serves 4.

–RICE PUDDING WITH PEACHES–

850 ml (30 fl oz/3¾ cups) full-fat milk
6 cardamom pods
115 g (4 oz/½ cup) short grain rice
55 g (2 oz/½ cup) pistachio nuts, chopped
115 g (4 oz/½ cup) soft brown sugar
55 g (2 oz/¼ cup) butter, diced
2 egg yolks
400 g (14 oz) can peach halves, drained

Put the milk in a flameproof casserole. Add the cardamom pods, bring to the boil and simmer gently for 5 minutes. Remove the cardamom pods. Stir in the rice.

Return to the boil and simmer gently, stirring frequently, for 15-20 minutes, until the rice is tender and most of the liquid has been absorbed. Remove from the heat and stir in the pistachio nuts, half the brown sugar, butter and egg yolks. Leave to cool slightly. Preheat oven to 160C (325F/Gas 3).

Remove half the mixture from the casserole and set aside. Arrange the peaches on top of the rice in the casserole and cover with the remaining rice. Bake for 25 minutes. Preheat grill. Sprinkle the pudding with the remaining sugar and grill until the sugar melts and turns a deep golden brown. Serve.

Serves 6-8.

COFFEE BRULÉE

8 egg yolks
115 g (4 oz/½ cup) caster sugar
250 ml (9 fl oz/1 cup) full-fat milk
500 ml (18 fl oz/2 cups) double (thick) cream
1 teaspoon coffee essence
summer berries, to decorate
TOPPING:
55 g (2 oz/¼ cup) caster sugar

In a large bowl, beat together the egg yolks and sugar until light and foamy.

Put the milk, cream and coffee essence in a flameproof casserole. Heat gently but do not boil. Remove from the heat and leave to cool. Preheat oven to 150C (300F/Gas 2). Pour the milk mixture on to the egg yolk mixture and stir well. Pour into a large jug and allow the froth to rise to the surface. Skim off the froth. Pour the mixture back into the casserole.

Put a piece of greaseproof paper in a roasting tin. Put the casserole on top of the paper. Pour enough boiling water into the tin to come halfway up the sides of the casserole. Bake for 45 minutes, until the mixture has set. Leave to cool then chill. To make the topping, preheat the grill. Sprinkle the top of the custard with the sugar and grill until the sugar melts and turns a deep golden brown. Decorate with summer berries and serve.

Serves 6.

WINTER FRUIT SALAD

115 g (4 oz) dried apricots
115 g (4 oz) dried apples
115 g (4 oz) prunes
50 g (2 oz) sultanas
50 g (2 oz) raisins
400 ml (14 fl oz/1¾ cups) unsweetened apple juice
2 x 5 cm (2 in) cinnamon sticks
1 pear, peeled, cored and quartered
thinly pared rind of ½ lemon

Put the dried fruit, apple juice and cinnamon sticks in a flameproof casserole. Cover and leave to soak for 12 hours.

Add the pear and lemon rind to the casserole. Bring to the boil and simmer gently for 15 minutes.

Remove the cinnamon sticks and strips of lemon rind. Serve warm or cold.

Serves 4-6.

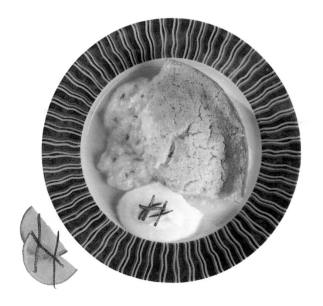

SAUCY LIME PUDDING

55 g (2 oz/¼ cup) unsalted butter, plus extra for
   greasing
55 g (2 oz/¼ cup) caster sugar
grated rind and juice of 3 limes
2 eggs, separated
55 g (2 oz/½ cup) self-raising flour
300 ml (10 fl oz/1¼ cups) milk

Preheat oven to 160C (325F/Gas 3). In a large
bowl, beat together the butter, sugar and lime
rind until light and fluffy. Stir in the egg
yolks and carefully fold in the flour. Stir in
the milk and lime juice.

Whisk the egg whites until they form stiff
peaks. Fold in to the lime mixture. Lightly
butter an ovenproof dish.

Pour the lime mixture into the dish and bake
for 40-50 minutes, until risen and golden.
Serve warm.

Serves 4-6.

──PRUNE & ALMOND TART──

225 g (8 oz) prunes
4 tablespoons brandy
225 g (8 oz) shortcrust pastry, thawed if frozen
115 g (4 oz/½ cup) unsalted butter, softened
115 g (4 oz/½ cup) icing sugar
3 eggs, beaten
55 g (2 oz/½ cup) plain flour
115 g (4 oz/½ cup) ground almonds
55 g (2 oz/½ cup) flaked almonds

Put the prunes and brandy in a bowl and leave to soak overnight. Roll out the pastry on a lightly floured surface and use to line a 27 cm (10½ in) flan dish.

Trim the pastry and prick the base all over with a fork. Drain the prunes and arrange in the pastry case. Preheat oven to 200C (400F/ Gas 6). In a bowl, beat together the butter and icing sugar. Beat in the eggs and fold in the flour and ground almonds. Spread the mixture evenly over the prunes.

Sprinkle the flaked almonds over the top. Bake for 40-45 minutes, until the filling is risen and golden brown. Serve warm.

Serves 6-8.

QUEEN OF PUDDINGS

500 ml (18 fl oz/2¼ cups) milk
55 g (2 oz/¼ cup) butter
115 g (4 oz/2 cups) cake crumbs
grated rind of 1 lemon
grated rind of 1 orange
55 g (2 oz/¼ cup) caster sugar
4 egg yolks, beaten
2 egg whites, whisked
55 g (2 oz) strawberry jam
115 g (4 oz) strawberries, sliced
icing sugar for dusting
MERINGUE:
2 egg whites
55 g (2 oz/¼ cup) caster sugar

Preheat oven to 160C (325F/Gas 3). Put the milk and butter in an ovenproof casserole and heat gently until the butter melts. Stir in the cake crumbs and lemon and orange rind. Add the sugar and egg yolks. Fold in the egg whites. Put the casserole in a deep roasting tin and pour in enough boiling water to come halfway up the sides of the casserole. Bake for 45-50 minutes, until set. Mix together the jam and strawberries and spread over the top of the pudding.

To make the meringue, beat the egg whites until they form stiff peaks. Fold in the sugar. Put the mixture in a piping bag and pipe in a trellis pattern on top of the pudding. Dust with icing sugar and bake (out of the roasting tin) for 30 minutes. Serve warm.

Serves 4-6.

INDEX